| 汉英对照 |

精准脱贫篇

Targeted Poverty Elimination

中国关键词

KEYWORDS TO UNDERSTAND CHINA

权 威 解 读 当 代 中 国

中国外文出版发行事业局（CIPG）
当代中国与世界研究院（ACCWS）
中国翻译研究院（CATL）

新世界出版社
NEW WORLD PRESS

First Edition 2020

Compiled by
China International Publishing Group
Academy of Contemporary China and World Studies
China Academy of Translation

Translated by
Han Qingyue

English text edited by
David W. Ferguson and Xu Mingqiang

Cover designed by
He Yuting

ISBN 978-7-5104-7140-7

Published by
NEW WORLD PRESS
24 Baiwanzhuang Street, Beijing 100037, China

Distributed by
NEW WORLD PRESS
24 Baiwanzhuang Street, Beijing 100037, China
Tel: 86-10-68995968
Fax: 86-10-68998705
Website: www.nwp.com.cn
E-mail: nwpcd@sina.com

Printed in the People's Republic of China

《中国关键词：精准脱贫篇》
编委会名单

前言

中共十八大以来，以习近平同志为核心的党中央站在全面建成小康社会、实现中华民族伟大复兴中国梦的战略高度，把脱贫攻坚摆到治国理政突出位置，提出一系列新思想新观点，作出一系列新决策新部署，推动中国减贫脱贫事业取得新成就。

消除贫困是人类共同的使命，是推动构建人类命运共同体的应有之义。中国在推进减贫脱贫实践中形成了许多重要经验和启示，为全球减贫事业贡献了中国智慧和中国方案。为增进国外读者对中国减贫脱贫事业的理解和认知，为国际减贫合作提供参考借鉴，“中国关键词多语对外传播平台”组织策划了《中国关键词：精准脱贫篇》。“中国关键词多语对外传播平台”由中国外文出版发行事业局、当代中国与世界研究院和中国翻译研究院联合组建运维，主要围绕习近平新时代中国特色社会主义思想，进行中文词条专题编写、解读以及多语种编译，通过平面、网络和移动社交平台等多媒体、多渠道、多形态及时持续对外发布，旨在以国外受众易于阅读和理解的方式，阐释中国理念和中国思想，解读中国政策和中国发展道路。

本篇围绕中国脱贫攻坚的重大理念和贫困治理的重要实践，从八个方面进行介绍和解读。我们深知，中国脱贫攻坚力度之大、规模之广、影响之深前所未有，很难用近百个词条将其讲清楚、讲完善、讲准确，加之编写和翻译团队时间紧、任务重，中文编写和外文编译内容难免有不尽如人意之处，我们真诚地欢迎大家批评指正。

讲故事需要关键词，讲好中国故事需要中国关键词。让我们用“中国关键词”点击中国、沟通世界。

Introduction

Since the 18th National Congress of the Communist Party of China in 2012, the Central Committee with Xi Jinping at its core has placed a high priority on poverty elimination in state governance, as part of the endeavors to complete the process of building a moderately prosperous society and realize the Chinese Dream of national rejuvenation. They have put forward a range of new ideas and philosophies and made decisions and arrangements designed to reduce and eliminate poverty in China.

Eliminating poverty is a shared mission of humanity, and an imperative for building a global community with a shared future. China has accumulated a wealth of experience in poverty reduction, and sharing this experience with others may provide inspiration to global endeavors in poverty elimination. For this purpose, this booklet, *Keywords to Understand China: Targeted Poverty Elimination*, is compiled.

China's poverty elimination endeavors are unprecedented in momentum, scale and influence, and it is hard to display the whole picture in approximately 100 keywords – the contents of this book. Due to the scope of the work and its tight schedule, oversights and inaccuracies are possible in our selection of entries. Our translations may also leave room for improvement. Comments and suggestions are welcome for future revisions.

The contents, divided into eight sections, are based on the "China Keywords" entries included in an eponymous multilingual platform. The "China Keywords" platform offers an authoritative guide to understanding contemporary China, and a window into China's political thinking, policies, and approach to development, including Xi Jinping Thought on Socialism with Chinese Characteristics for a New Era.

A major national project implemented and operated by the China International Publishing Group, the Academy of Contemporary China and World Studies, and the China Academy of Translation, the multilingual platform can be accessed online and on mobile social media platforms.

Keywords are at the heart of any story. "China Keywords" are at the heart of the story of China. We hope that the project will help build a bridge of understanding between China and the rest of the world.

Contents
目　录

决胜脱贫攻坚，共享全面小康
Winning the Final Battle Against Poverty to Achieve Moderate Prosperity for All

第一个百年奋斗目标
The First Centenary Goal 002

“四个全面”战略布局
The Four-Pronged Comprehensive Strategy 006

“五位一体”总体布局
The Five-Sphere Integrated Plan...... 010

“四个意识”
The “Four Consciousnesses” 014

共同富裕
Common Prosperity 018

人的全面发展
The Universal Development of the Individual 022

先富帮后富
Those Who Become Prosperous First Helping Those Who Lag Behind..026

脱贫攻坚战
The Battle Against Poverty..............030

打赢脱贫攻坚战三年行动
The Three-Year Action Plan for Poverty Elimination.........................034

绝对贫困
Absolute Poverty...........................038

相对贫困
Relative Poverty.............................040

贫困代际传递
Intergenerational Transmission of Poverty.......................................042

贫困发生率
Poverty Headcount Ratio................046

区域性整体贫困
Overall Regional Poverty.................048

全面建成小康社会
Completing the Building of a Moderately Prosperous Society in All Respects..............................052

以脱贫攻坚统揽经济社会发展全局
Overall Economic and Social Development Through Poverty Elimination 056

供给侧结构性改革
Supply-Side Structural Reform 060

生态保护扶贫
Ecological Conservation for Poverty Alleviation 064

现行标准下农村贫困人口实现脱贫
Eliminating Poverty Among Rural People Living Below the Current Poverty Line 066

两不愁三保障
Two Assurances and Three Guarantees 070

解决区域性整体贫困
Eliminating Overall Regional Poverty 074

整体消除绝对贫困现象
Eliminating Absolute Poverty 076

悬崖效应
"Abyss Consequence" 078

坚持党的领导，强化组织保证
CPC Leadership and Organizational Guarantee

井冈山精神
The Spirit of the First Revolutionary Base in the Jinggang Mountains...... 084

坚持党对脱贫攻坚的领导
The CPC Leadership over Poverty Elimination 086

“五级书记”
CPC Secretaries at Five Levels Responsible for Poverty Elimination.. 090

强化党政一把手负总责
Top CPC and Government Leaders Responsible for Poverty Elimination.. 094

政治优势
Political Strengths 098

制度优势
Institutional Strengths 102

中央扶贫开发工作会议
The Central Conference on Poverty Alleviation and Development 106

党建促扶贫
Strengthening Party Development in Poverty Alleviation......................... 110

"最后一公里"
The "Last-Mile" Problem 114

坚持精准方略，提高脱贫实效

Employing Targeted Poverty Elimination to Achieve Anticipated Results

贫困地区
Impoverished Areas......................... 120

深度贫困地区
Severely Impoverished Areas 124

"三区三州"
The Most Impoverished Three Regions and Three Prefectures 128

"直过民族"
"Ethnic Groups with Cross-Stage Development"................................ 130

贫困县
Poor Counties 132

贫困村
Poor Villages 136

贫困户
Poor Households 140

整村推进
Village-Based Poverty Alleviation 142

十八洞村
Shibadong Village 144

补短板
Improving Areas of Weakness 148

问题导向
Problem-Oriented Approaches 152

精准扶贫
Targeted Poverty Alleviation............. 156

“四个问题”
Four Key Issues in Poverty
Alleviation 160

建档立卡
Poverty Registration 164

“回头看”
Follow-Up Checks 168

“五个一批”
Five Measures for Poverty
Elimination 170

“六个精准”
Six Elements of Targeted Poverty
Alleviation 174

“七个强化”
Seven Aspects of Reinforcing
Poverty Alleviation Work.................. 178

因地制宜
Acting According to Local Conditions 182

因户施策
Targeted Measures for Each Household 186

综合施策
Holistic Approaches to Poverty Elimination 190

贫困县全部摘帽
Lifting All Poor Counties Out of Poverty 192

摘帽不摘政策
Poverty Relief Policies Continue After Counties Being Removed from Poverty List. 196

驻村帮扶
Resident Work Teams in Poor Villages.. 198

决胜脱贫攻坚，
共享全面小康

Winning the Final Battle Against Poverty to Achieve Moderate Prosperity for All

第一个百年奋斗目标

20世纪80年代，中国共产党提出“三步走”的社会主义现代化建设战略目标：第一步，到20世纪80年代末，实现国民生产总值比1980年翻一番，解决人民的温饱问题；第二步，到20世纪末，使国民生产总值再增长一倍，人民生活达到小康水平；第三步，到21世纪中叶，人均国民生产总值达到中等发达国家水平，人民生活比较富裕，基本实现现代化。

在解决人民温饱问题、人民生活总体上达到小康水平这两个目标基础上，中国共产党提出“两个一百年”的奋斗目标。第一个百年奋斗目标：到建党100年时建成经济更加发展、民主更加健全、科教更加进步、文化更加繁荣、社会更加和谐、人民生活更加殷实的小康社会。第二个百年奋斗目标：到新中国成立100年时，基本实现现代化，把中国建成社会主义现代化国家。

全面建成小康社会，实现第一个百年奋斗目标，一个标志性的指标是农村贫困人口全部脱贫。中共十八大以来，党中央

The First Centenary Goal

In the 1980s the CPC devised a three-step strategic plan for modernization. The first step was to double the 1980 gross national production (GNP) by the end of the 1980s and ensure that the whole population would have adequate food and clothing. The second step was to further double the 1990 GNP by the end of the 20th century and ensure the people a moderately prosperous life. The third step was to increase the per capita GNP level to that of moderately developed countries, ensure the people a relatively affluent life, and achieve basic modernization by the middle of the 21st century.

Having attained the first two of these three goals, the CPC set itself two new goals, known as the Two Centenary Goals.

The first goal calls for completing the building of a moderately prosperous society by the time the CPC celebrates its centenary in 2021, when China will have a stronger economy, greater democracy, more advanced science and education, more thriving culture, greater social harmony, and a better quality of life.

The second goal is to achieve basic modernization and turn China into a modern socialist country by the time the People's Republic of China celebrates its centenary in 2049.

从全面建成小康社会要求出发，把扶贫开发工作纳入“五位一体”总体布局、“四个全面”战略布局，作为实现第一个百年奋斗目标的重点任务，作出一系列重大部署和安排，全面打响脱贫攻坚战。

A defining indicator in attaining the first goal is lifting all rural residents living below the current poverty line out of poverty. Since 2012, the year when the 18th CPC National Congress was convened, the central leadership has made poverty alleviation and development a major part of the Five-sphere Integrated Plan and the Four-pronged Comprehensive Strategy, and rolled out a series of policies for the final nationwide battle of poverty elimination.

“四个全面”战略布局

2014年12月，习近平在江苏省调研时，首次将全面建成小康社会、全面深化改革、全面依法治国、全面从严治党这“四个全面”并提。2015年2月，习近平在中央党校省部级主要领导干部研讨班开班式上，明确肯定“四个全面”是“战略布局”，并且第一次用“战略布局”来概括中共十八大以来党中央治国理政的总体框架。

“四个全面”战略布局是从中国发展现实需要中得出来的，是从人民群众的热切期待中得出来的，是为推动解决中国面临的突出矛盾和现实问题提出来的，适应了中国发展的时代需要。“四个全面”战略布局，既有战略目标又有战略举措，每一个“全面”都蕴含着重大战略意义，相互之间密切联系、有机统一，具有紧密的内在逻辑，是一个整体战略部署的有序展开，共同支撑起中国特色社会主义事业全局。全面建成小康社会是重大战略目标，在“四个全面”战略布局中居于引领地位。全面深化改革、全面依法治国、全面从严治党是三大战略举措，为如期全面建成小康社

The Four-Pronged Comprehensive Strategy

During an inspection tour in Jiangsu Province in December 2014, Xi Jinping talked for the first time about the Four-pronged Comprehensive Strategy, which consists of completing the building of a society which is moderately prosperous in all respects, comprehensively expanding in-depth reform, comprehensively promoting law-based governance, and comprehensively enforcing strict Party self-governance.

Speaking to the provincial officials attending a training session at the Central Party School in February 2015, he called this a Four-pronged Comprehensive Strategy, which he used to summarize the governance framework of the CPC Central Committee since its 18th National Congress.

This Four-pronged Comprehensive Strategy was formulated to help solve the most pressing problems and issues currently facing the country. It caters to the needs of the real conditions in China.

The four prongs are closely linked. Together they support the overall development of Chinese socialism. Completing the building of a moderately prosperous society in all respects is the strategic goal and foremost element of the Four-pronged Comprehensive

会提供重要保障。三大战略举措对实现全面建成小康社会战略目标一个都不能缺。“四个全面”战略布局，是中国共产党在新形势下治国理政的总方略，是事关党和国家长远发展的总战略，为实现“两个一百年”奋斗目标、实现中华民族伟大复兴的中国梦提供了重要保障。习近平多次指出，全面建成小康社会，关键是要把经济社会发展的“短板”尽快补上，否则就会贻误全局。其中，最艰巨最繁重的任务在农村，特别是在贫困地区，这是全面建成小康社会最大的“短板”，脱贫攻坚由此被纳入“四个全面”战略布局。

Strategy. The other three are strategic measures that support the goal.

The Four-pronged Comprehensive Strategy is an important guarantee for realizing the Two Centenary Goals and the Chinese Dream of national rejuvenation.

Xi Jinping reiterates that to build a moderately prosperous society in all respects, the areas of weaknesses in economic and social development must be improved; otherwise, there will be a significant impact on the whole process. The toughest and heaviest task is to help rural areas, poor areas in particular, which are the weakest areas in the country. Poverty elimination is thus part of the Four-pronged Comprehensive Strategy.

“五位一体”总体布局

2012年11月8日，中共十八大提出经济建设、政治建设、文化建设、社会建设、生态文明建设“五位一体”的建设中国特色社会主义总体布局。即在坚持以经济建设为中心的同时，全面推进经济建设、政治建设、文化建设、社会建设、生态文明建设，促进现代化建设各个环节、各个方面协调发展。“五位一体”总体布局和“四个全面”战略布局相互促进、彼此联动，旨在以推动经济发展为基础，统筹建设社会主义市场经济、民主政治、先进文化、和谐社会、生态文明，协同推进人民富裕、国家强盛、中国美丽。“五位一体”总体布局的提出，体现了中国共产党对协调发展的规律性认识不断深化，对中国特色社会主义的规律性认识不断深化。

脱贫攻坚纳入“五位一体”总体布局，不仅意味着脱贫攻坚战要为推进经济建设、政治建设、文化建设、社会建设、生态文明建设补齐短板，同样也意味着要将“五位一体”总体布局的要求贯彻于脱贫攻坚战全过程。在各地脱贫攻坚实践中，产

The Five-Sphere Integrated Plan

The Five-sphere Integrated Plan – the development of socialism with Chinese characteristics encompassing economic, political, cultural, social and eco-environmental development – was proposed on November 8, 2012 at the 18th National Congress of the CPC. While economic development continues to be the central pillar, economic, political, cultural, social and eco-environmental development is to be promoted on all fronts, modernization is to be fostered in all sectors, and all elements are to be developed in a coordinated manner.

The Five-sphere Integrated Plan and the Four-pronged Comprehensive Strategy support each other and interact in a planned manner. Proceeding from economic growth, they help develop a socialist market economy, democratic governance, advanced culture, and a harmonious society with eco-environmental progress. Together, they help make the people more prosperous, the country stronger, and the landscape more beautiful.

Efforts made in these five spheres are also reflected in China's poverty elimination campaign, so as to boost economic, political, cultural, social, and eco-environmental progresses. In the poverty elimination process,

业扶贫、党建扶贫、文化扶贫、社会扶贫和生态扶贫等一系列创新举措，都深刻地体现了“五位一体”总体布局的要求。

new measures are adopted to create more jobs for poverty-stricken people, give full play to CPC organizations and members in poverty alleviation programs, and organize cultural, social and eco-environmental activities for the needy.

“四个意识”

2016年1月29日，中共中央政治局召开会议，首次公开提出“增强政治意识、大局意识、核心意识、看齐意识”。“四个意识”的提出，标志着中国政治、中国治理进入一个新阶段，以习近平同志为核心的党中央，将以更大的责任与担当，带给中国民众更多获得感。

“四个意识”是一个有机的整体。强化政治意识，要求坚定理想信念，坚定对马克思主义的信仰，始终坚持正确的政治方向，在思想上、政治上、行动上同党中央保持高度一致；强化大局意识，要求正确处理全局与局部的关系，时刻不要忘记整

The "Four Consciousnesses"

On January 29, 2016, the Political Bureau of the CPC Central Committee publicly spelled out for the first time the "Four Consciousnesses":

- maintaining political integrity;
- thinking in terms of the broader picture;
- following the leadership core; and
- keeping in alignment with the CPC Central Committee.

These requirements for CPC members represent a new stage in China's governance. The CPC Central Committee with Xi Jinping at the core will take more responsibilities and heavier tasks to let the Chinese people have a sense of gain from the development.

The "Four Consciousnesses" are closely interconnected. The consciousness of the need to maintain political integrity means that CPC members are always firm in their convictions and Marxist belief, follow a correct political orientation, and stay in close unison with the Central Committee in thought and deed.

The consciousness of the need to think in terms of the broader picture means that CPC members balance the relationships between national and regional conditions, with the overall interest in mind.

The consciousness of the need to

体利益；强化核心意识，要求在工作中抓住重点问题，时刻不要忘记党和人民的需求；强化看齐意识，要求在实践中与党中央保持高度一致，任何时候都不能偏离正确方向。

follow the leadership core means that CPC members focus on major issues and always remember the needs of the Party and the people.

The consciousness of the need to keep in alignment means that CPC members always follow the Central Committee and never deviate from the correct direction.

共同富裕

马克思提出，在新的社会制度中“社会生产力的发展将如此迅速”，“生产将以所有的人富裕为目的”。恩格斯在描述社会主义时也指出，“我们的目的是要建立社会主义制度，这种制度将给所有的人提供健康而有益的工作，给所有的人提供充裕的物质生活和闲暇时间，给所有的人提供真正的充分的自由”。

中国共产党自诞生之日起，就以消除贫困、改善民生、实现共同富裕为使命，谋求通过建立社会主义制度而从根本上消灭贫困问题。邓小平在不同场合多次提及共同富裕，他指出，社会主义与资本主义不同的特点就是共同富裕，不搞两极分化。在改革中，我们始终坚持两条根本原则，一是以社会主义公有制经济为主体，一是共同富裕。走社会主义道路，就是要逐步实现共同富裕。共同致富，我们从改革一开始就讲，将来总有一天要成为中心课题。社会主义不是少数人富起来、大多数人穷，不是那个样子。社会主义最大的优越性就是共同富裕，这是体现社会主义本质的一个东西。

对于坚持共同富裕这一社会主义理

Common Prosperity

In describing his prediction of a new social system [of socialism], Karl Marx said that the development of the social productive forces would grow so rapidly and that production would be calculated for the wealth of all. In the words of Frederick Engels, "Our aim is to bring about a Socialist System which will give healthy and useful labor to all, ample wealth and leisure to all, and the truest and fullest freedom to all."

From its very beginning, the CPC has taken eliminating poverty, improving wellbeing and achieving common prosperity as its mission, and worked to end poverty fundamentally through development of socialism. Deng Xiaoping had more than once talked about common prosperity:

"One of the features distinguishing socialism from capitalism is that socialism means common prosperity, not polarization of income...."

"In the reform we have consistently followed two fundamental principles. One is the predominance of the socialist public sector of the economy; the other is common prosperity...."

"To take the road to socialism is to realize common prosperity step by step...."

"Since the very beginning of the reform we have been emphasizing the need for seeking common prosperity; that will surely

想，习近平明确指出：“共同富裕是中国特色社会主义的根本原则，所以必须使发展成果更多更公平惠及全体人民，朝着共同富裕方向稳定前进。”脱贫攻坚战正是实现这一理想的必由之路。只有补齐了经济社会发展的“短板”，中国特色社会主义事业才能一往无前，共同富裕的理想目标才能最终实现。

be the central issue someday. Socialism does not mean allowing a few people to grow rich while the overwhelming majority live in poverty. No, that's not socialism. The greatest superiority of socialism is that it enables all the people to prosper, and common prosperity is the essence of socialism."

Regarding the socialist goal of common prosperity, Xi Jinping pointed out, "Common prosperity is the fundamental principle of Chinese socialism – this is why we must ensure that all the people share the fruits of development in a fair way, and move steadily toward common prosperity." The battle against poverty is a pathway toward this goal.

人的全面发展

马克思指出，作为社会主体的每一个人在个性、道德、能力等方面的和谐、自由、全面的发展和完善，是共产主义的社会理想和人类的理想，与人的片面的、畸形的发展相对。马克思在创立历史唯物主义时提出了这一思想，在《共产党宣言》中以“自由人的联合体”来描述共产主义的社会理想，后来又在《资本论》及其他经济学著作中多次提出“全面而自由的发展”目标。

马克思主义不仅从现实的“平等主义”角度论证了“一切人”的发展，也从个体的角度提出了“人的全面发展”的社会理想，即“使社会的每一个成员都能完全自由地发展和发挥他的全部才能和力量，并且不会因此而危及这个社会的基本条件”。在这个意义上，消除贫困成为人的全面发展的基本要求。社会主义不仅要让人们实现温饱的目标，更要使人民过上能够全面发展的美好生活。以“人的全面发展”为目标，意味着消除贫困不仅是解除贫困人

The Universal Development of the Individual

Karl Marx pointed out that harmonious, free and comprehensive development and improvement of every member of society in their individuality, virtue and capacity is the social ideal and aspiration of all humanity and communism, which is different from imbalanced development favoring particular individuals. He put forward this idea when he created the theory of historical materialism. He used "a community of free individuals" to describe the social ideal of communism in the *Manifesto of the Communist Party*, and mentioned the goal of "comprehensive and free development" in *Capital* and other works on economics.

Marxism advocates the development of all individuals on an equal footing and the comprehensive development of human beings, "To organize society in such a way that every member of it can develop and use all his capabilities and powers in complete freedom and without thereby infringing the basic conditions of this society." In this sense, ending poverty is the basic requirement for the universal development of individuals. Socialism will not only ensure people's basic needs – food and clothing – but also bring them a better life with universal development.

口的经济约束，更要实现他们对美好生活的向往。因此，习近平要求，坚持以促进人的全面发展的理念指导扶贫开发，丰富贫困地区文化活动，加强贫困地区社会建设，提升贫困群众教育、文化、健康水平和综合素质，振奋贫困地区和贫困群众精神风貌。

To end poverty and pursue “universal development” will relieve the people of their economic bonds and realize their desire for a better life. Xi Jinping urges promoting people’s well-rounded development to guide poverty alleviation endeavors, increasing cultural activities and social programs in poor areas, enhancing education, culture, and healthcare services for local people, and improving their moral standards.

先富帮后富

改革开放之前，人民生活水平提高缓慢，社会主义的优越性未能充分体现出来。为了充分显示社会主义的优越性，就必须首先让人们生活富裕。但是，一些错误观念严重束缚着人们的思想，制约了生产力的发展。为此，邓小平当时提出了“先富带动共富”的政策理念，意在调动人民群众的积极性和创造性。邓小平指出，我们提倡一部分地区先富裕起来，是为了激励和带动其他地区也富裕起来，并且使先富裕起来的地区帮助落后的地区更好地发展。提倡人民中有一部分人先富裕起来，也是同样的道理。一部分地区、一部分人可以先富起来，带动和帮助其他地区、其他的人，逐步达到共同富裕。

脱贫攻坚战中，东西部扶贫协作和对口支援集中体现了“先富帮后富”的思想，是推动区域协调发展、协同发展、共同发

Those Who Become Prosperous First Helping Those Who Lag Behind

Prior to China's era of reform and opening up, the Chinese people saw only a slow improvement in their living conditions, and socialism was not fully showing its superiority. To demonstrate the strengths of socialism, China needed to achieve common prosperity. But at that time some erroneous ideas still fettered people's thinking and hampered the productive forces.

Seeing this, Deng Xiaoping proposed encouraging those who have become prosperous first to inspire others to follow their example. He said, "In encouraging some regions to become prosperous first, we intend that they should inspire others to follow their example and that all of them should help economically backward regions to develop. The same holds good for some individuals," and "some regions and some people may prosper before others do, and then they can help other regions and people to gradually do the same."

This idea is fully applied in China's battle against poverty, particularly in the cooperation and paired-up assistance between the east and the west. It helps promote regional

展的大战略，是加强区域合作、优化产业布局、拓展对内对外开放新空间的大布局，是最终实现共同富裕目标的大举措。

cooperation for coordinated development, with a better industrial configuration and more space for opening to the rest of the country and the world, with the final goal of common prosperity.

脱贫攻坚战

改革开放40多年来，中国经济社会发展取得巨大成就，几亿贫困人口脱贫，完成这期间全世界超过70%的减贫任务。中共十八大以来，中国通过实施精准扶贫、精准脱贫，加大扶贫投入，创新扶贫方式，推动扶贫开发工作呈现新局面。2013年至2019年，中国连续7年超额完成千万减贫任务。7年间，全国累计减少贫困人口9348万人，贫困发生率从10.2%下降到0.6%，创造了中国扶贫史上的最好成绩。中国成为世界上减贫人口最多的国家，也是世界上率先完成联合国千年发展目标的国家。但中国的脱贫攻坚形势依然严峻。截至2019年年底，全国农村贫困人口约551万人，其中相当一部分居住在艰苦边远地区，处于深度贫困状态，属于脱贫攻坚“最重的担子”“最硬的骨头”。

让贫困人口和贫困地区同全国一道进

The Battle Against Poverty

Since the launch of reform and opening up in 1978, China has made great economic and social progress. The hundreds of millions of people that China has lifted out of poverty account for over 70 percent of global poverty reduction during the period.

Since the 18th CPC National Congress, China has implemented targeted poverty alleviation and elimination measures, increased input in poverty alleviation programs, and found new ways to achieve results.

From 2013 to 2019, China fulfilled its yearly goals of poverty reduction and helped a total of 93.5 million people emerge from poverty, and the poverty headcount ratio dropped from 10.2 percent to 0.6 percent. All of these represent remarkable achievements.

China has helped more people out of poverty than any other country. It is also the first country in the world to complete the UN Millennium Goal. However, the task remains tough. By the end of 2019, there were 5.5 million people still living in poverty, a significant number of whom lived in remote places or border regions under harsh natural conditions. These represent a significant challenge.

Ensuring that poor people and poor areas enjoy moderate prosperity together with

入全面小康社会，是中国共产党的庄严承诺。中共十九大报告提出坚决打赢脱贫攻坚战，要求动员全党全国全社会力量，坚持精准扶贫、精准脱贫，坚持中央统筹、省负总责、市县抓落实的工作机制，强化党政一把手负总责的责任制，坚持大扶贫格局，注重扶贫同扶志扶智相结合，深入实施东西部扶贫协作，重点攻克深度贫困地区脱贫任务，确保到2020年中国现行标准下农村贫困人口实现脱贫，贫困县全部摘帽，解决区域性整体贫困，做到脱真贫、真脱贫。

the rest of the country is a solemn promise made by the CPC. The CPC set the task of winning the battle against poverty in its report to the 19th National Congress. It demanded greater efforts to mobilize the energies of the whole Party, the whole country, and the whole of society, and continue to implement targeted poverty alleviation and elimination measures. China will continue the working mechanism whereby the central leadership makes overall plans, provincial authorities take overall responsibility, and city and county authorities ensure implementation, and it will strengthen the system for making heads of Party committees and governments at all levels assume overall responsibility for poverty alleviation.

Poverty alleviation is an all-encompassing campaign. China will pay particular attention to helping people develop confidence in their own ability to lift themselves out of poverty, and ensure that they can acquire necessary knowledge and skills in order to succeed. It will strengthen collaboration on poverty alleviation between the eastern and western regions, and provide focused assistance to areas of extreme poverty.

By the year 2020, three targets must be reached – all rural residents living below the current poverty line are lifted out of poverty, all poor counties get rid of poverty, and overall regional poverty is eliminated. Poverty alleviation should reach those who truly need it and deliver genuine outcomes.

打赢脱贫攻坚战三年行动

中共十九大明确把精准脱贫作为决胜全面建成小康社会必须打好的三大攻坚战之一，作出了新的部署。从脱贫攻坚任务看，2018至2020年，还有3000万左右农村贫困人口需要脱贫，其中因病、因残致贫比例居高不下，在剩余3年时间内完成脱贫目标，任务十分艰巨。中共中央、国务院针对这些突出问题，印发了《中共中央 国务院关于打赢脱贫攻坚战三年行动的指导意见》，对完善顶层设计、强化政策措施、加强统筹协调，推动脱贫攻坚工作更加有效开展作出全面部署，为各地各部门深入推进脱贫攻坚工作提供了基本遵循。

《指导意见》明确了打赢脱贫攻坚战三年行动的工作要求，提出必须做到“7个坚持”，也就是：坚持严格执行现行扶贫标准；坚持精准扶贫精准脱贫基本方略；坚持把提高脱贫质量放在首位；坚持扶贫同扶志扶智相结合；坚持开发式扶贫和保

The Three-Year Action Plan for Poverty Elimination

Poverty elimination was announced as one of the three critical battles (the other two being forestalling and defusing major risks and the prevention and control of pollution) that the CPC vowed to win at its 19th National Congress held in October 2017. About 30 million rural residents are to be lifted out of poverty between 2018 and 2020. This is really a tough task to fulfill within three years, given the large number of people who live in poverty because of illness and disability.

Targeting these problems, the central leadership in June 2018 released a Three-year Guideline on Winning the Battle Against Poverty, providing top-level design, supporting policies and measures, and guidance on coordinating efforts in different localities and government departments.

Detailed tasks are designated in the document, which demands that:

(1) The current criteria for poverty alleviation be applied;

(2) Both targeted poverty alleviation and elimination be followed;

(3) Top priority be given to improving the quality of poverty alleviation work;

(4) The disadvantaged population can acquire necessary knowledge and skills to

障性扶贫相统筹；坚持脱贫攻坚与锤炼作风、锻炼队伍相统一；坚持调动全社会扶贫积极性。

escape poverty with more confidence;

(5) Development-oriented poverty alleviation be carried out and the basic living needs of rural poor population be met;

(6) The skills of workers assigned to poverty alleviation work be enhanced; and

(7) The whole of society be mobilized to contribute.

绝对贫困

绝对贫困的“绝对”有两个方面的含义：一是指界定贫困的尺度是绝对的，它以维持或满足人的基本生存或基本需要为参照标准；二是指贫困的程度较深，处于绝对匮乏或剥夺状态。在发展中国家，绝对贫困一般又称为生存贫困或基本需要贫困，或者说，绝对贫困包含生存贫困或基本需要贫困两个层次。度量个人或家庭是否处于绝对贫困状态，其基本方法是由国家或社会设定一条民众可接受的能满足最低限度基本生存或基本需要的物质福利标准（即绝对贫困线），然后将个人或家庭的实际福利水平（收入或消费）与绝对贫困线相比较，处于贫困线下的个人或家庭就确定为绝对贫困人口或家庭。确定绝对贫困线的方法，主要有标准预算法、恩格尔系数法、马丁法等。

Absolute Poverty

Absolute poverty has two criteria: First, the baseline for poverty is absolute; it refers to the basic living standards or basic needs for human subsistence. Second, it means a condition of extreme poverty, with a severe shortage of basic necessities of life or extreme deprivation of basic human needs. Absolute poverty is also called "subsistence poverty" or "basic needs poverty" in some developing countries.

To determine whether an individual or family is living under absolute poverty, an acceptable wellbeing line (absolute poverty line) is set for basic needs or minimum living conditions for subsistence, and the individual or family will be defined as suffering absolute poverty if their wellbeing (income or consumption) falls below this line.

There are a number of ways to define the absolute poverty line, such as the Market Basket Method, Engle's Ratio Method and Martin Method.

相对贫困

与绝对贫困对应的概念是相对贫困。相对贫困是建立在将穷人的生活水平与其他不太贫困的社会成员的生活水平相比较的基础上的，通常这包括对作为研究对象的社会总体平均水平的测度。相对贫困有三个特征：第一，它是一种由社会作出的主观判断。其实际上是社会上多数人对于较低生活水平的一定确认，如有的国家以全国人均收入的一定比例作为贫困标准，而有的国家则以中位收入水平的一定比例作为贫困标准。第二，它具有历史动态性。随着不同时期的社会生产力和生活方式的变化，贫困标准也有很大差别。第三，它具有长期性。相对贫困的实质是不平等，只要社会存在不平等，就存在相对贫困，实际上，由于不平等是常态，因而相对贫困也将普遍存在。

2020年全面建成小康社会之后，中国将整体消除绝对贫困，但相对贫困仍将长期存在。到那时，针对绝对贫困的脱贫攻坚举措要逐步调整为针对相对贫困的日常性帮扶措施，并纳入乡村振兴战略架构下统筹安排。

Relative Poverty

Relative poverty is the result of comparing the living standards of poor people and those of other members of the society. It reveals the overall living conditions of a society as a whole.

Relative poverty has three features:

(1) It is a subjective judgment made by a society, or the majority of the residents, about lower living standards. Some countries take a certain percentage of the per capita income as the poverty threshold, while others use a certain percentage of the median income as the benchmark.

(2) It is a concept that evolves. Over time the baseline for poverty may vary due to changes in social productivity and ways of life.

(3) It is protracted in nature. Relative poverty is in essence inequality. As long as inequality exists, there is relative poverty. Since inequality always exists, relative poverty will exist everywhere.

Absolute poverty will be eliminated in China by 2020, as the country becomes moderately prosperous in all respects. But relative poverty will remain for a long time. Then the measures taken to tackle absolute poverty will gradually evolve into routine assistance to those living in relative poverty, and become part of the rural revitalization strategy.

贫困代际传递

贫困代际传递是指贫困以及导致贫困的相关条件和因素，在家庭内部由父母传递给子女，使子女在成年后重复父母的境遇——继承父母的贫困和不利因素并将贫困和不利因素传递给后代的恶性遗传链；也指在一定的社区或阶层范围内，贫困以及导致贫困的相关条件和因素在代际之间延续，使后代重复前代的贫困境遇。

教育是阻断贫困代际传递的治本之策。目前，一些贫困地区的教育发展面临很大困难，由于各种原因，贫困家庭孩子辍学失学还比较多，“读书无用论”观点也有所蔓延，不少贫困家庭子女受教育程度同普通家庭的差距正在扩大。贫困地区教育事业是管长远的，必须下大气力抓好。脱贫攻坚期内，职业教育培训是工作重点。一个贫困家庭的孩子如果能接受职业教育，掌握一技之长并顺利就业，这一户

Intergenerational Transmission of Poverty

Intergenerational transmission of poverty is a vicious circle under which conditions and factors that cause poverty are passed down from parents to children, who will inherit these same conditions and factors and pass them down to their children. The phenomenon can also exist in particular communities or social strata, and thus poverty is passed down from generation to generation.

Education is an effective way to prevent intergenerational transmission of poverty. At present, impoverished areas face difficulties in education, and there are many school dropouts from poor families. The idea that "education is useless" is widespread among such people. The gap between the education of children from poor families and that from ordinary families is widening. Education has far-reaching significance to the poor regions, and needs to be addressed with great effort.

Vocational education and training are essential to China's poverty elimination before 2020. If children from underprivileged households can receive vocational education and acquire some skills for future employment, their families will have better prospects of escaping poverty.

National education funds will continue to be weighted toward poor regions, for basic

脱贫就有希望了。国家教育经费要继续向贫困地区倾斜、向基础教育倾斜、向职业教育倾斜，特岗计划、国培计划同样要向贫困地区基层倾斜。要帮助贫困地区改善办学条件，加大支持乡村教师队伍建设力度，建立省级统筹乡村教师补充机制。要探索率先从建档立卡的贫困家庭学生开始实施普通高中教育免学（杂）费，落实中等职业教育免学（杂）费，大城市优质学校同贫困地区学校结对等帮扶政策。要对农村贫困家庭幼儿特别是留守儿童给予特殊关爱，探索建立贫困地区学前教育公共服务体系。

and vocational education, as will the state training program for special posts and national teachers' training program. The conditions of schools in poor areas will be improved, rural teachers will receive more support, and a mechanism will be put in place whereby the provincial government will coordinate the replenishment of rural teachers. Senior high school students from families registered as living under the poverty line will be the first to be exempt from tuition and related fees, students of secondary vocational schools will also be exempt from tuition and related fees, and schools with good education resources in major cities will be paired up with those in poor regions to provide assistance to the latter. Particular care will be given to preschool children of rural poor families and left-behind children whose parents are working away from home, and a system for public services will be set up for preschool education in impoverished areas.

贫困发生率

贫困发生率又称“贫困人口指数”，指国家或地区生活在贫困线以下的贫困人口数量占总人口之比。由于贫困发生率对于一个国家或地区的贫困状况的表述较为直观，因此不仅有助于考察国家或地区贫困状况，而且是检验减贫政策有效性的重要指标。

在脱贫攻坚战中，贫困发生率不仅是贫困村识别的重要指标，即“行政村贫困发生率比全省贫困发生率高一倍以上”，也是贫困县脱贫摘帽的主要衡量标准，即“贫困发生率必须低于2%（西部地区低于3%）”。改革开放40多年来，中国农村7亿多贫困人口摆脱贫困，贫困发生率由1978年的97.5%下降到2018年年底的1.7%，创造了人类减贫史上的中国奇迹。

Poverty Headcount Ratio

The poverty headcount ratio is the ratio of the number of people living under the poverty line in a country or a region to the total population. It is an objective reflection of poverty in a country or a region, and it is a major norm for evaluating the poverty reduction policy.

In China, if the poverty headcount ratio of a village is more than double that of the province where it is located, it will be identified as impoverished, and if the poverty headcount ratio of a county is lower than 2 percent, it will be regarded as having eliminated poverty. In western areas this figure is 3 percent.

Since China launched reform and opening up in the late 1970s, more than 700 million poor people have been lifted out of poverty, and the poverty headcount ratio has been cut from 97.5 percent in 1978 to 1.7 percent in late 2018, a true miracle in the history of poverty reduction.

区域性整体贫困

2011年发布的《中国农村扶贫开发纲要（2011—2020年）》大致指出了中国连片特困地区的范围：国家将六盘山区、秦巴山区、武陵山区、乌蒙山区、滇桂黔石漠化区、滇西边境山区、大兴安岭南麓山区、燕山—太行山区、吕梁山区、大别山区、罗霄山区等区域的连片特困地区和已明确实施特殊政策的西藏、四省藏区、新疆南疆三地州，作为扶贫攻坚主战场。中国在解决区域性整体贫困问题方面的主要理念和实践是：第一，始终坚持以经济建设为中心，坚持发展是硬道理，把发展作为解决中国所有问题的关键和中国共产党执政兴国的第一要务。第二，将生存权和发展权作为首要的基本人权。第三，在

Overall Regional Poverty

In the Outline for Development-oriented Poverty Alleviation of China's Rural Areas (2011-2020), released in 2011, the following are identified as contiguous areas of extreme poverty: Liupan Mountains, Qinling-Bashan mountains, Wuling Mountains, Wumeng Mountains, desertified regions in Yunnan, Guangxi and Guizhou, border mountainous regions in west Yunnan Province, regions at the southern foot of the Greater Hinggan Mountains, Yanshan-Taihang mountains, Lüliang Mountains, Dabie Mountains, and Luoxiao Mountains, as well as the Tibet Autonomous Region, the Tibetan ethnic areas in Sichuan, Yunnan, Gansu and Qinghai provinces, and the three prefectures in southern Xinjiang (Hotan, Kashi and the Kizilsu Kirgiz Autonomous Prefecture) where special poverty alleviation policies have been applied already.

The following are the Chinese visions for eliminating regional poverty:

(1) Focusing on economic development as the central task and regarding development as the top priority and as the key to solving all issues in China and to improving the CPC's governance;

(2) Considering the rights to subsistence and development as the primary human rights;

具体推进国家和社会发展中，有计划、分阶段、稳扎稳打地解决贫穷问题。第四，长期以来坚持有重点地解决贫穷问题。虽然中国脱贫攻坚目标是在2020年解决区域性整体贫困问题，但是在防止返贫、缓解相对贫困、缩小发展差距方面，依然任重道远。

(3) Advancing poverty alleviation in a planned manner, step by step; and

(4) Tackling poverty with priorities.

The country is expected to eliminate overall regional poverty by the year 2020, but after that there will be the challenges of preventing people from slipping back into poverty, relieving relative poverty, and narrowing the development gap.

全面建成小康社会

改革开放之初，邓小平首先用“小康”来诠释中国式现代化，明确提出到20世纪末“在中国建立一个小康社会”的奋斗目标。在这个基础上，中共十六大提出本世纪头20年全面建设惠及十几亿人口的更高水平的小康社会的目标。中共十七大提出了全面建设小康社会的新要求。中共十八大对全面建设小康社会目标进行了充实和完善，将“全面建设小康社会”调整为“全面建成小康社会”。全面小康，覆盖的领域要全面，是五位一体全面进步的小康。全面小康，覆盖的人口要全面，是惠及全体人民的小康。全面小康，覆盖的区域要全面，是城乡区域共同发展的小康。全面建成小康社会，要求实事求是，因地制宜。

Completing the Building of a Moderately Prosperous Society in All Respects

The goal of establishing a moderately prosperous society by the end of the 20th century was raised by Deng Xiaoping in the late 1970s and early 1980s, when the roadmap for China's modernization was being devised.

In its report to the 16th National Congress in 2002, the CPC Central Committee called for a continued push to build a moderately prosperous society in all respects in the first 20 years of the 21st century. New and more ambitious elements were subsequently added to this expanded concept at the Party's 17th National Congress in 2007. In its report to the 18th National Congress in 2012, the CPC Central Committee announced the goal of completing the process of building a moderately prosperous society in all respects by the year 2020.

A moderately prosperous society in all respects is one with progress in the economic, political, cultural, social and eco-environmental spheres, with all the people being covered and sharing the fruits of development, and with moderate prosperity in both urban and rural areas. In building

中共十八大以来，小康社会的内涵进一步扩展。习近平将扶贫开发与党和政府的职责、党的根本宗旨以及全面建成小康社会的目标要求和社会主义的本质要求相结合，深刻阐述中国现阶段扶贫开发的极端重要性和紧迫性。中共十八届五中全会明确提出，确保到2020年中国现行标准下农村贫困人口全部脱贫。中共十九大报告也对全面建成小康社会作出了明确部署。

全面建成小康社会，是“两个一百年”奋斗目标中的第一个百年奋斗目标，是中华民族伟大复兴征程上的重要里程碑，在“四个全面”战略布局中居于引领地位。

such a society, approaches applicable to local conditions are to be taken.

Since 2012, the definition of "a moderately prosperous society" has further expanded. Xi Jinping defines poverty alleviation as the mission of the CPC and the government, and calls poverty elimination a salient requirement of socialism, thus highlighting the extreme importance and urgency of poverty alleviation in present-day China.

At its fifth plenary session held in October 2015, the 18th CPC Central Committee announced the goal of helping all rural residents living below the current poverty line out of poverty by 2020. The CPC at its 19th National Congress in 2017 set a clear goal for completing the building of a moderately prosperous society in all respects. This is the first of the Two Centenary Goals, and will be a milestone in the journey toward national renewal. It is the foremost element of the Four-pronged Comprehensive Strategy.

以脱贫攻坚统揽经济社会发展全局

脱贫攻坚不仅是要使贫困人口如期全部脱贫，还要使贫困地区经济社会发展上一个台阶。习近平指出，深度贫困地区党委和政府要坚持把脱贫攻坚作为“十三五”期间的头等大事和第一民生工程来抓，坚持以脱贫攻坚统揽经济社会发展全局。

脱贫攻坚不仅要围绕贫困人口脱贫做工作，同样要以区域经济社会全面发展为前提。精准扶贫的实践不仅是中国社会政策领域的创新，同时也包含了区域经济发展的创新。随着脱贫攻坚的深入，原有贫困县不断脱贫摘帽，县域经济社会发展迈上了新台阶。在精准扶贫实践的进程中，不仅县域发展的基础设施与公共服务水平有了较大提升，地方政府的治理能力也得到了锻炼，为经济社会可持续发展奠定了良好基础。在脱贫摘帽县中，一些地方不仅彻底摆脱了贫困县的帽子，而且形成了

Overall Economic and Social Development Through Poverty Elimination

The goals of China's poverty elimination campaign are to lift all disadvantaged people out of poverty as scheduled, and to bring local economic and social development to a higher level. Xi Jinping has demanded that the local authorities and Party committees in severely impoverished areas take poverty elimination their top priority and the most important project for improving people's wellbeing during the 13th Five-year Plan period (2016-2020). They should focus on poverty elimination in local overall social and economic development.

As well as helping the impoverished population, regional development also deserves great attention. Targeted poverty alleviation is a Chinese innovation in social policy and in regional economic development. As more and more poor counties succeed in eliminating poverty, their economic and social development has been raised to a new level. Infrastructure and public services have been improved, and the local governments' governance capability has been enhanced, thus laying a solid foundation for sustainable development. Some of these counties, once

良好的产业格局和经济环境。

以脱贫攻坚统揽经济社会发展全局，要重点以县域经济社会发展为基础。习近平指出，县级党委是全县脱贫攻坚的总指挥部，县委书记要统揽脱贫攻坚，统筹做好进度安排、项目落地、资金使用、人力调配、推进实施等工作。

very poor, now have a much better industrial configuration and economic environment.

County social and economic development is the foundation for national development. As Xi Jinping says, county CPC committees should be the headquarters of the poverty elimination campaign, and country Party committee secretaries should take overall charge of poverty elimination – coordinating schedules, launching projects, allocating funds, assigning personnel, and promoting the implementation of projects.

供给侧结构性改革

习近平指出，供给侧结构性改革“重点是解放和发展社会生产力”，“既强调供给又关注需求，既突出发展社会生产力又注重完善生产关系，既发挥市场在资源配置中的决定性作用又更好发挥政府作用，既着眼当前又立足长远”。自2015年首次提出之后，供给侧结构性改革成为当前中国经济工作的核心，其手段方法也伴随着中国社会经济的发展而变化：从2015年强调“三去一降一补”，到2017年强调重点在“破、立、降”上下功夫，再到2018年提出要在“巩固、增强、提升、畅通”八个字上下功夫。推进供给侧结构性改革，是以习近平同志为核心的党中央在综合分析世界经济长周期和中国发展阶段性特征及其相互作用的基础上，集中全党和全国人民智慧，从理论到实践不断探索的结晶。其不仅在理论上丰富了经济新常态理论，为中国特色社会主义政治经济学书写了新篇章，而且在实践上开创了中

Supply-Side Structural Reform

According to Xi Jinping, the key to supply-side structural reform is to release and develop productive forces. The reform focuses on both supply and demand, aims to develop productive forces and improve relations of production, allows the market to play its decisive role in resource allocation and the government to better fulfill its functions, and looks to address both present and future needs. An idea first proposed in 2015, supply-side structural reform is the current priority in China's economic work.

China has adopted different policies to proceed with the reform in tandem with its economic and social development. In 2015, the reform focused on "cutting overcapacity and excess inventory, deleveraging, reducing costs, and tackling areas of weaknesses"; in 2017, the emphasis was on "cutting ineffective supply, fostering new growth drivers, and reducing costs"; and in 2018 the attention was on "consolidating, strengthening, upgrading, and ensuring unimpeded flows."

Supply-side structural reform reflects the theory and practice of the CPC Central Committee with Xi at its core, based on an overall analysis of the world economic cycle and the features of China's development, and the interaction between them. It enriches

国改革发展、宏观调控和经济结构调整的新纪元。供给侧结构性改革也为打赢脱贫攻坚战、促进贫困地区加快发展提供了科学指引。

China's vision of the new normal economy and the socialist political economy with Chinese features, and also heralds a new era in the country's reform and opening up, macro regulation, and economic structural adjustment. Supply-side structural reform guides China's battle against poverty while accelerating the development of poor areas.

生态保护扶贫

绿水青山就是金山银山，是习近平反复强调的生态文明建设理念。这一思想理念，蕴含着对人类文明发展经验教训的历史总结，体现着对人类发展意义的深刻思考，破解了发展中人对物质利益的追求与人赖以生存的生态环境的关系这一难题，彰显了当代中国共产党人高度的文明自觉和生态自觉。牢固树立“绿水青山就是金山银山”的理念，就是把生态保护放在优先位置，实现绿色发展。扶贫开发不能以牺牲生态为代价，必须探索生态脱贫新路子，让贫困人口从生态建设与修复中得到更多实惠。

生态保护扶贫包括两大核心思想：一是在贫困地区实施可持续型、环境友好型扶贫开发项目，最大限度地帮助地区经济实现发展，做到对生态环境不伤害、不破坏。二是将生态环境看成是一种能够得到有效利用的扶贫资源加以开发，从而实现当地经济发展、人民生活水平提高和生态环境保护的高度统一。

Ecological Conservation for Poverty Alleviation

"Lucid waters and lush mountains are invaluable assets" – this is a philosophy Xi Jinping cherishes on environmental protection and eco-environmental conservation. Based on his summation of the lessons and experiences of human development, it reflects Xi's profound thinking about civilization. It is an approach to development that balances the pursuit of material benefits with protection of the eco-environment in which we exist. It also shows that the Party values development that respects environmental protection.

Acting on this understanding, people will give priority to conservation and pursue green development. Poverty alleviation must not proceed at the expense of the environment. New approaches will be explored so that the poor will benefit from eco-environmental conservation and restoration.

Guided by this philosophy, sustainable and environment-friendly development projects are supported in poor regions to boost the local economy without causing damage to the environment, and the eco-environment will itself be developed as a resource in a way to ensure local economic development, improve local living conditions and protect the eco-environment at the same time.

现行标准下农村贫困人口实现脱贫

2015年发布的《中共中央 国务院关于打赢脱贫攻坚战的决定》明确提出脱贫攻坚总体目标：到2020年，稳定实现农村贫困人口不愁吃、不愁穿，义务教育、基本医疗和住房安全有保障；确保中国现行标准下农村贫困人口全部脱贫，消除绝对贫困；确保贫困县全部摘帽，解决区域性整体贫困。

现行标准是指结合“三保障”措施制定的稳定温饱标准。在“三保障”的前提下，现行标准包括的食物支出比重（即恩格尔系数）为53.5%，按农产品出售和购买综合平均价，在农村地区每人每天消费1斤米面、1斤蔬菜和1两肉或1个鸡蛋。在此基础上，现行标准还包括保障一定数量的非食品支出，满足与健康生存同等重要的衣、住、用、行以及义务教育、基本医疗等需求，从而实现“不愁吃、不愁穿”的稳定温饱要求。扶贫标准每年按农村贫

Eliminating Poverty Among Rural People Living Below the Current Poverty Line

According to the Decision on Winning the Battle Against Poverty, promulgated in 2015, the overall goals set by the central leadership for poverty elimination are: by 2020, the rural poor will have adequate food and clothing and access to compulsory education, basic medical services and safe housing; all rural poor population (defined as those living below current poverty line) will be lifted out of poverty and absolute poverty be eradicated; all impoverished counties will be free of poverty, and overall regional poverty will have been eliminated.

The current poverty line is a standard set to meet the people's basic needs of food and clothing. Specifically, the Engel's Coefficient (the proportion of income spent on food) of the poor population is 53.5 percent, and each rural resident has 500 grams of rice or flour, 500 grams of vegetables, and 50 grams of meat or one egg per day. A certain amount of non-food expenditure is also guaranteed to meet people's needs for clothing, housing, daily expenses, travel, compulsory education and basic medical services. The standard will be updated based on the yearly price index

困人口面对的物价指数更新。

打赢脱贫攻坚战，有着明确的时间节点和攻坚目标。在实践中，要坚持现行脱贫标准，既不拔高，也不降低。

affecting the rural poor.

China has a clear timetable and realistic goals for its battle against poverty. The current standard will neither be raised nor lowered.

两不愁三保障

习近平指出，到2020年稳定实现农村贫困人口不愁吃、不愁穿，义务教育、基本医疗、住房安全有保障，是贫困人口脱贫的基本要求和核心指标，直接关系攻坚战质量。

“两不愁”是要稳定解决农村贫困人口的温饱问题。与过去“有吃、有穿”的要求相比，现行标准还可满足健康生存需要的热量和蛋白质需求，做到贫困人口“吃饱，适当吃好”。

“三保障”是要提高农村人口的发展和抗风险能力，为稳定解决温饱创造条件。实现义务教育有保障主要是让贫困家庭义务教育阶段的孩子不失学；实现基本医疗有保障主要是所有贫困人口都参加医疗保险制度，常见病、慢性病有地方看、看得起，得了大病、重病后基本生活过得去；

Two Assurances and Three Guarantees

China's poverty relief goals are as follows: by 2020, the rural poor will be assured of adequate food and clothing, and guaranteed access to compulsory education, basic medical services and safe housing. These are better known in China as "two assurances and three guarantees." They are the basic requirements and the core evaluation metrics on which victory in the battle against poverty is directly dependent.

The "two assurances" will resolve the problems of food and clothing for impoverished rural people. Compared with the previous goal of meeting people's basic needs for food and clothing, the current standard guarantees people's needs for adequate calories and protein for good health, that is, they will not only have food to eat, but also eat properly.

The "three guarantees" will help enhance the rural population's ability to offset risks and develop, and will create conditions for steadily resolving their problems of food and clothing.

Access to compulsory education means that children will not drop out of school because of inadequate family finances; access to basic medical services means that all impoverished people will be covered by medical insurance, that they can afford to see a doctor in the case of common and chronic diseases, and that their lives will not deteriorate

住房安全有保障，主要是让贫困人口不住危房。此外，还要保障饮水安全，让农村人口喝上放心水。

“两不愁三保障”具有稳定性含义。教育、健康、住房都是管长远的，实现“三保障”意味着奠定了稳定的脱贫机制。

severely should they suffer serious or critical diseases; access to safe housing means that disadvantaged people will no longer live in sub-standard houses. Rural residents will also be guaranteed access to safe drinking water.

The "two assurances and three guarantees" are of great significance to individuals in the long run. If these are met, it indicates that a sound mechanism for stable poverty elimination is in place.

解决区域性整体贫困

解决区域性整体贫困，是中共十八届五中全会明确2020年打赢脱贫攻坚战的一项目标任务。就是以习近平关于扶贫开发的重要思想为根本遵循，围绕“四个全面”战略布局，牢固树立并切实贯彻创新、协调、绿色、开放、共享的发展理念，充分发挥政治优势和制度优势，把精准扶贫、精准脱贫作为基本方略，坚持扶贫开发与经济社会发展相互促进，坚持精准帮扶与集中连片特殊困难地区开发紧密结合，坚持扶贫开发与生态保护并重，坚持扶贫开发与社会保障有效衔接，咬定青山不放松，采取超常规举措，拿出过硬办法，举全党全社会之力，确保国家现行标准下农村贫困人口实现脱贫，贫困县全部摘帽，完成解决区域性整体贫困的底线任务。

Eliminating Overall Regional Poverty

Eliminating overall regional poverty is one of the goals for 2020, set by the 18th CPC Central Committee at its fifth plenary session in 2015.

Guided by Xi Jinping's thought on poverty alleviation, China has followed the Four-pronged Comprehensive Strategy, implementing an innovative, coordinated, green, open and shared approach to development. It has leveraged its political and institutional strengths and taken targeted measures in poverty alleviation. It advances poverty alleviation in tandem with economic and social progress, coordinates targeted poverty alleviation with the development of contiguous poverty-stricken areas, and gives equal emphasis to poverty alleviation and eco-environmental conservation. It also coordinates poverty alleviation with social security programs.

With firm determination, unique intensity, and effective measures, China has mobilized efforts and resources nationwide and Party-wide to ensure that all those living below the current poverty line are lifted out of poverty, that all poor counties get rid of poverty, and that overall regional poverty is eliminated as scheduled.

整体消除绝对贫困现象

打好精准脱贫攻坚战是中共十九大提出的三大攻坚战之一。中共十八届五中全会从实现全面建成小康社会奋斗目标出发，明确了到2020年国家现行标准下农村贫困人口实现脱贫，贫困县全部摘帽，解决区域性整体贫困。由此，到2020年国家现行标准下农村贫困人口实现脱贫，成为中国共产党对中国人民作出的庄严承诺。届时，中华民族在几千年发展史上，将首次整体消除绝对贫困现象。这对中华民族、对整个人类都具有重大意义。

Eliminating Absolute Poverty

Poverty elimination is one of the three critical battles the CPC vowed to win at its 19th National Congress. The goals were specified at the fifth plenary session of the 18th CPC Central Committee in October 2015: to raise out of poverty all those living below the current poverty line, to lift all poor counties out of poverty, and eliminate overall regional poverty, all by the year 2020.

To raise all those living under the current poverty line out of poverty by 2020 – this is a solemn promise made by the CPC. At this point the Chinese nation will have eliminated absolute poverty for the first time in its history. This will be significant to China and to the whole of humanity.

悬崖效应

在脱贫攻坚实践中，一些地方自觉不自觉地把扶贫标准拔高，甚至不同地区之间互相攀比看谁的标准高，对贫困户做了一些不切实际的承诺，设置的地方性考核指标明显超过了“两不愁三保障”标准。这些做法使得贫困户和非贫困户待遇差距太大，出现“悬崖效应”。一些地方对贫困村、贫困县的退出，规定了很多硬性的验收指标，验收指标也存在层层加码的问题，有些指标确实与“两不愁三保障”，以及基本公共服务主要领域指标接近全国平均水平没有太直接的关系。这导致为了完成这些硬性指标，一些贫困县确实尽力而为，但是没有量力而行，甚至不惜举债搞贫困村建设，有的贫困村一次性就投入一两千万元资金，贫困村和非贫困村出现了“悬崖效应”。

对于这些问题，2018年发布的《中共中央 国务院关于打赢脱贫攻坚战三年行动的指导意见》明确要求，脱贫攻坚要量力

"Abyss Consequence"

In poverty elimination, some localities have intentionally or inadvertently raised their poverty thresholds, and some have even tried to compete with others in their standards, making irrational promises to impoverished households. As a result, their local assessment norms have come to exceed the national standards for basic living needs and for access to compulsory education, basic medical services and safe housing. This has led to an unreasonable gap between poverty-stricken households and other villagers, which is known as the "abyss consequence."

Some localities have set irrational standards for poverty elimination in poor villages and poor counties, while at each level the standards are raised in evaluation. This is irrelevant to the national standards for poverty elimination and to the main indicators of basic public services. To meet such mandated requirements, some poor counties try their best, but it is beyond their actual capacity. Some even borrow funds to support their poor villages. In the worst case, 10 million to 20 million yuan has been invested in one poor village, thus creating an "abyss consequence" between poor villages and non-poor villages.

Addressing these problems, the Three-year Guideline on Winning the Battle Against Poverty, issued by the central leadership in 2018, demands that poverty elimination must

而行，既不能降低标准，也不能擅自拔高标准、提不切实际的目标，避免陷入“福利陷阱”，防止产生贫困村和非贫困村、贫困户和非贫困户待遇的“悬崖效应”，留下后遗症。

be pragmatic. The standards shall neither be randomly lowered nor irrationally raised, so as to avoid the “welfare trap” and the “abyss consequence” between poor and non-poor villages and between poor and non-poor households, and other unfavorable consequences.

坚持党的领导，
强化组织保证
CPC Leadership and Organizational Guarantee

井冈山精神

1927年，中国共产党在江西省建立了第一块农村根据地——井冈山革命根据地，开辟了“以农村包围城市、武装夺取政权”的革命道路，井冈山也因此成为中国革命的摇篮。从此，井冈山被载入了中国革命历史史册，井冈山精神也在此得到孕育和发展。

井冈山精神内涵丰富，坚定信念、艰苦奋斗是其灵魂，实事求是、敢闯新路是其核心，依靠群众、勇于胜利是其根本。井冈山精神最重要的价值之一，在于其开辟了中国革命的独特道路，拉开了中国革命新时期的序幕。正是传承了这种不怕苦、不怕累、不怕牺牲的井冈山精神，革命老区的人民才通过自己的双手，一步步坚定地走在脱贫致富的道路上。

The Spirit of the First Revolutionary Base in the Jinggang Mountains

In 1927, after the failure of its urban uprising, the CPC established its first revolutionary base in the Jinggang Mountains in Jiangxi Province. From there it began to organize the peasantry to encircle the cities from the rural areas and seize political power through armed struggle. The Jinggang Mountains thus became the cradle of Chinese revolution.

The Jinggang Mountains spirit is characterized by perseverance and a belief in achieving victory through armed struggle. The significance of this spirit is that it helped the CPC find its own road to revolution.

Carrying on the unyielding spirit of the revolutionary pioneers, the people living in this old revolutionary base area have developed a spirit of self-reliance, and through hard work they are marching toward prosperity.

坚持党对脱贫攻坚的领导

消除贫困就是中国共产党的初心和使命，不同历史时期，党都领导人民以不同方式不断为实现这一目标而努力。中共十八大以来，脱贫攻坚被纳入“五位一体”总体布局和“四个全面”战略布局进行部署，党对于脱贫攻坚的领导得以不断强化，党的领导力、组织力和战斗力得以充分运用于打赢脱贫攻坚战。

党对于脱贫攻坚的总体把握，确保了脱贫攻坚的方向不偏移，强化了党是脱贫攻坚的政治保证这一根本认识。特别是在脱贫攻坚任务重的地区，党委和政府始终把脱贫攻坚作为“十三五”期间头等大事和第一民生工程来抓，坚持以脱贫攻坚统揽经济社会发展全局，充分发挥各级扶贫开发领导小组的作用，加强扶贫机构队伍建设。党组织体系是脱贫攻坚的组织载体，

The CPC Leadership over Poverty Elimination

Eliminating poverty is part of the CPC's mission and aspiration. In different historic periods, the CPC has led the people to work for this goal in different ways.

Since 2012, poverty elimination has been incorporated into China's Five-sphere Integrated Plan and Four-pronged Comprehensive Strategy. The CPC leadership over the campaign has been reinforced, and the CPC's leadership and mobilization capacity have been fully leveraged to ensure victory in the fight against poverty.

The Party's overall command keeps the poverty elimination campaign on the right course and provides a solid political guarantee for achieving the final goal. In places where poverty elimination work is tough, local authorities and Party committees take poverty elimination their top priority and the most important project for improving people's wellbeing during the 13th Five-year Plan period (2016-2020). They focus on poverty elimination in overall social and economic development. The poverty alleviation leading groups at all levels attend to their role, build effective mechanisms, and create a contingent of competent personnel.

Party organizations, grassroots branches in particular, are the organizational

尤其是基层党组织的作用突出。正所谓“农村要发展，农民要致富，关键靠支部”。

2015年中央扶贫开发工作会议以来，脱贫攻坚顶层设计基本完成，“五级书记”抓扶贫、全党动员促攻坚的格局基本形成，各项决策部署得到较好贯彻落实，精准扶贫、精准脱贫深入人心。

medium for carrying out poverty elimination work. Village Party branches are key to rural development and to the common prosperity of rural residents.

Following the Central Conference on Poverty Alleviation and Development in 2015, the top-level strategy for poverty elimination has been completed. A structure has been built with Party secretaries at five levels in charge and the whole Party mobilized, and relevant planning and measures have been implemented. Targeted poverty alleviation and elimination have gained extensive support across the country.

“五级书记”

中国共产党的领导是中国脱贫攻坚最大的政治优势。“五级书记”是指省、市、县、乡四级党委书记和村党支部书记。脱贫攻坚是省市县乡村五级书记一起抓的一把手工程，是一项极其重大、极为严肃的政治任务。

中共中央决定，脱贫攻坚任务重的省区市的党政一把手签订脱贫攻坚责任书，向中央作出承诺，并且要层层落实责任，省市县乡村五级书记一起抓扶贫。同时，应充分发挥贫困地区和贫困人口作为脱贫攻坚主体的作用。贫困人口的脱贫、贫困地区的发展，需要党和政府的帮助，需要各方面的支持，但最终还是要靠自身努力。必须激发贫困地区、贫困人口的内生动力，鼓励他们自力更生、艰苦奋斗、勤劳致富、自强不息，在国家政策支持下，在各方面支持下，靠自己的双手改变贫穷面貌，改变落后的命运。

习近平强调，要把实施乡村振兴战略摆在优先位置，坚持五级书记抓乡村振兴，让乡村振兴成为全党全社会的共同行动。通

CPC Secretaries at Five Levels Responsible for Poverty Elimination

The CPC leadership is China's biggest political strength in its poverty elimination effort. The five levels refer to the Party committees of provinces, cities (prefectures), counties and townships, and the Party branches of villages. For Party secretaries at these five levels, poverty elimination is a serious political task that they must take on the responsibility to fulfill.

The CPC Central Committee has decided that in places with challenging poverty elimination work, the heads of provincial-level Party committees and governments will assume overall responsibility and sign written pledges to the central leadership, and they and their subordinates at all levels will be responsible for poverty alleviation under their jurisdiction.

Poor people and poor regions will play a key role in poverty elimination. In addition to assistance from the CPC, the government and other social sectors, they need to rely on themselves. They must be inculcated with an internal drive to better themselves.

Xi Jinping emphasizes giving top priority to the rural revitalization strategy, and having Party secretaries at five levels take charge of the implementation. The vision is to

过实现乡村产业振兴、人才振兴、文化振兴、生态振兴、组织振兴，推动农业全面升级、农村全面进步、农民全面发展。

promote the overall upgrading of agriculture and progress of rural areas and farmers through developing economic activities, cultural progress, and eco-environmental conservation.

强化党政一把手负总责

实现农村贫困人口脱贫，贫困县全部摘帽，是打赢“十三五”脱贫攻坚战、决胜全面建成小康社会的第一目标。党政一把手作为“管总”的负责人，责无旁贷。习近平对于“一把手责任”多次进行论述强调，加强领导是根本，要发挥各级党委领导作用，建立并落实脱贫攻坚一把手负责制，实行省市县乡村五级书记一起抓，为脱贫攻坚提供坚强政治保障。要强化中央统筹、省负总责、市县抓落实的工作机制，强化党政一把手负总责的责任制，强化县级党委作为全县脱贫攻坚总指挥部的关键作用。各级党政干部特别是一把手，必须增强政治担当和责任担当，以高度的历史使命感亲力亲为抓好脱贫攻坚工作。

脱贫攻坚战以来，各地各部门通过签署扶贫“军令状”、严格扶贫工作政绩考核、实施“扶贫一把手工程”等方式，不断强化“一把手责任”。“党政一把手负总责”体现了脱贫攻坚战的重要地位，要求

Top CPC and Government Leaders Responsible for Poverty Elimination

To lift all people and counties out of poverty is the goal in China's efforts to build a society of moderate prosperity in all respects. Heads of Party committees and governments at all levels must not shirk from their overall responsibility to achieve this goal. Xi Jinping has elaborated on this, highlighting heads of Party committees and governments, their responsibilities and the role of CPC secretaries at five levels in policy implementation.

The working mechanism requires that the central leadership makes overall plans, provincial authorities take overall responsibility, and city and county authorities ensure implementation. This mechanism will be reinforced, as will the system for making heads of Party committees and governments at all levels assume overall responsibility for poverty elimination, and the key role of county Party committees as the general command in the battle. These officials must take on their political duties and tasks with a strong sense of historic mission.

各级党委和政府高度重视扶贫开发工作，将扶贫开发列入重要议事日程，摆在更加突出的位置。“党政一把手负总责”也彰显了脱贫攻坚的政治优势与制度优势，脱贫攻坚正以前所未有的力度不断推进，取得历史性成就。此外，强化“党政一把手负总责”既需要加大扶贫工作问责力度，也需要加强对扶贫领域违法违纪问题的查处。

With the introduction of poverty elimination pledges and strict evaluation of their performance, the "first-in-commands" now have a strong awareness of their responsibilities. The emphasis on their duties also mirrors the importance of the battle against poverty, and relevant political and institutional strengths. Accountability will be correspondingly tightened up, and violations of law and discipline will be punished.

政治优势

坚持党的领导，发挥社会主义制度可以集中力量办大事的优势，这是中国的最大政治优势。实现贫困人口如期脱贫，是中国共产党向全国人民作出的郑重承诺。责任重于泰山，各级党委和政府必须不辱使命。

推进脱贫攻坚工作，要坚持把人民利益放在首位，各级领导干部要从巩固党执政的阶级基础和群众基础、保持党同人民群众血肉联系的高度出发，增强推进脱贫攻坚工作的使命感和责任感。要充分发挥政治优势，形成推进脱贫攻坚工作的强大合力。脱贫攻坚工作，是中国共产党的历史使命，是各级党委、政府和各部门一把手的职责。实施党政一把手脱贫攻坚工作责任制、脱贫攻坚期内保持贫困县党政正

Political Strengths

CPC leadership and the efficiency of socialism in pooling resources to solve major problems – these are the biggest political strengths of China. To raise all poor population out of poverty as planned is a solemn promise made by the CPC to the whole Chinese nation. Taking on weighty responsibilities, Party committees and governments at all levels must live up to the expectations of the people.

In China's poverty elimination campaign, the interests of the people are placed first. For the purpose of consolidating the class foundation, achieving popular support for the CPC's governance, and maintaining its close ties with the people, officials are required to have a greater sense of mission and responsibility in their work, give play to the political strengths of the system, and build synergy in poverty elimination.

As poverty elimination is the historic mission undertaken by the CPC, the "first-in-commands" of Party committees and governments and their departments at every level are responsible for poverty elimination under their jurisdiction. During the critical phase of the battle against poverty in impoverished counties, county Party committee secretaries and county mayors will remain steadfast in their posts. Eastern areas are paired up with areas

职稳定、开展东西部扶贫协作和机关定点扶贫、向贫困村派驻第一书记和驻村工作队等行之有效的措施，必须继续坚持，不断提高水平。

in the west in cooperative programs, and central departments have designated targets of assistance. First Party secretaries and resident working teams have been dispatched to poor villages to help with the poverty alleviation work. These measures have been followed and proved effective in China's poverty alleviation effort.

制度优势

人民当家作主是社会主义民主政治的本质特征。中国是工人阶级领导的、以工农联盟为基础的人民民主专政的社会主义国家，国家一切权力属于人民。习近平指出，中国社会主义民主是维护人民根本利益的最广泛、最真实、最管用的民主。发展社会主义民主政治就是要体现人民意志、保障人民权益、激发人民创造活力，用制度体系保证人民当家作主。

中国共产党从成立之日起就以实现人民当家作主为己任，团结带领中国人民进行新民主主义革命，为争取民族独立、人民解放，实现人民当家作主不懈奋斗。新中国成立后，中国共产党领导人民建立了人民当家作主的国家政权，进行了广泛的民主实践，实现了中国从几千年封建专制政治向人民民主的伟大飞跃，开辟了人民当家作主的历史新纪元。改革开放40多年来特别是中共十八大以来，中国特色社会主义政治发展道路越走越宽广，人民当家作主的制度保障越来越健全，社会主义民主的优越性更加充分地展示出来。

Institutional Strengths

That the people are masters of the country is an essential feature of socialist democracy. China is a socialist country of people's democratic dictatorship under the leadership of the working class and based on an alliance of workers and farmers, and it is a country where all power of the state belongs to the people. As Xi Jinping says, China's socialist democracy is the broadest, most genuine, and most effective democracy to safeguard the fundamental interests of the people. The very purpose of developing socialist democracy is to give full expression to the will of the people, protect their rights and interests, spark their creativity, and provide systemic and institutional guarantees to ensure that the people run the country.

From the very beginning, the CPC has striven to ensure the position of the people as masters of the country. It united and led the Chinese people in the New Democratic Revolution in pursuit of national independence and liberation and making the people masters of the country.

After the People's Republic was founded in 1949, the CPC led the people in establishing a state power with the people as masters of the country and building extensive democracy, thus realizing China's great transition from a millennia-old feudal autocracy to a people's democracy.

党政军机关、企事业单位开展定点扶贫，是中国特色扶贫开发事业的重要组成部分，也是中国政治优势和制度优势的重要体现。

Since the late 1970s when China began reform and opening up, and especially since 2012, socialist democracy with Chinese features has advanced on a broad front. Institutions to ensure the people's position as masters of the country have been improved, and socialist democracy is demonstrating its great strengths.

The practice of having CPC and government departments, the military, enterprises and public institutions paired up with poor counties to provide assistance to the latter is an important part of China's poverty elimination campaign. It demonstrates the political and institutional strengths of China.

中央扶贫开发工作会议

2015年11月27日至28日，中央扶贫开发工作会议在北京召开。这次中央扶贫开发工作会议是中共十八届五中全会后召开的第一个中央工作会议，体现了党中央对扶贫开发工作的高度重视。会议的主要任务是，贯彻落实中共十八届五中全会精神，分析全面建成小康社会进入决胜阶段面临的形势和任务，对当前和今后一个时期脱贫攻坚任务作出部署，动员全党全国全社会力量，齐心协力打赢脱贫攻坚战。

中共中央总书记、国家主席、中央军委主席习近平出席会议并发表重要讲话。他强调，消除贫困、改善民生、逐步实现共同富裕，是社会主义的本质要求，是中国共产党的重要使命。全面建成小康社会，是对全国人民的庄严承诺。脱贫攻坚战的冲锋号已经吹响。要立下愚公移山志，咬定目标、苦干实干，坚决打赢脱贫

The Central Conference on Poverty Alleviation and Development

On November 27-28, 2015, the Central Conference on Poverty Alleviation and Development was held in Beijing. This was the first central conference following the fifth plenary session of the 18th CPC Central Committee the previous October. It showed the Central Committee's strong commitment to poverty alleviation.

The major tasks of this conference were to implement the decision of the fifth plenary session, analyze the current conditions, map out work in the final period of achieving moderate prosperity in all respects, make present and future plans to carry out the work required, and mobilize all forces of the Party and the nation to win the battle against poverty.

Speaking to the conference, Xi Jinping pointed out that eliminating poverty, improving living standards, and achieving common prosperity is a fundamental task for socialism and an important mission of the CPC. Building a moderately prosperous society in all respects is the CPC's promise to the people. A clarion call was sounded in the battle against poverty. To win this battle, officials must have firm resolve and clear goals, and work hard with a down-to-earth spirit, to bring

攻坚战，确保到2020年所有贫困地区和贫困人口一道迈入全面小康社会。讲话中，习近平对脱贫攻坚的重要性和艰巨性、打赢脱贫攻坚战面临的矛盾和问题进行了深刻的分析，系统阐明了精准扶贫、精准脱贫基本方略，为打赢脱贫攻坚战提供了根本遵循。

moderate prosperity to all poverty-stricken areas and individuals by 2020.

Xi also offered a profound analysis of the importance and urgency of poverty elimination, and the problems and difficulties in winning the battle against poverty. He elaborated on the strategy of targeted poverty alleviation and elimination, and provided guidance on winning the national battle against poverty.

党建促扶贫

抓好党建促扶贫，是贫困地区脱贫致富的重要经验。习近平提出要贯彻落实“围绕扶贫抓党建，抓好党建促扶贫，检验党建看脱贫”的理念。农村基层党组织是党在农村全部工作和战斗力的基础，是贯彻落实党的扶贫开发工作部署的战斗堡垒。要把扶贫开发同基层组织建设有机结合起来，抓好以村党组织为核心的村级组织配套建设，把基层党组织建设成为带领乡亲们脱贫致富、维护农村稳定的坚强领导核心，发展经济、改善民生，建设服务型党支部，寓管理于服务之中，真正发挥战斗堡垒作用。

在脱贫攻坚领域，抓党建促扶贫凸显了中国国家贫困治理体系的政治优势，加强和改善党的领导为打赢脱贫攻坚战提供了强有力的政治保障和组织保障。首先，脱贫攻坚，涉及众多的行动主体，通过加强党的领导形成统一的认识、统一的行动，有利于集中各类资源，聚合积极力

Strengthening Party Development in Poverty Alleviation

Strengthening Party development in poverty alleviation is a gained experience of China. Xi Jinping has proposed the idea of making Party development and poverty elimination mutually reinforcing, and assessing Party development by the results of poverty elimination.

Rural grassroots Party branches are the bases of the Party's rural work, and they play a decisive role in implementing the Party's plans for development-oriented poverty alleviation. Poverty alleviation will advance with the development of grassroots organizations. Concurrently, village management organizations centered on village Party branches will be strengthened. Party branches will be the core that leads villagers to get rid of poverty, better themselves, and maintain rural stability. They will be service-oriented in serving the people, developing the local economy, and improving local living standards.

Promoting poverty elimination by strengthening Party development is an asset in China's poverty alleviation effort. Improving CPC leadership provides a powerful political and organizational guarantee for winning the war against poverty.

量，形成脱贫攻坚的广泛合力。其次，“一切为了人民，一切依靠人民，从群众中来，到群众中去”的工作路线和“实事求是”的思想路线，为各项扶贫开发政策的有效落实，提供了方向的指引和机制的保障。再次，通过动员“干部下乡”，促进国家精准扶贫各项政策在社区层面、农户层面有效落实，并将一线的信息迅速反馈到决策层面，为进一步优化各项政策提供了基础。同时，“干部下乡”在实践中历练，有助于干部自身的成长。最后，夯实基层组织建设，将贫困社区党组织建设成为带领村民，特别是贫困农户脱贫增收的“红色引擎”，在脱贫攻坚的过程中凝聚民心、民智、民力，密切干群关系，将增进农户对党和国家政策的认同，从而巩固党的执政基础。

First, poverty elimination involves many players, and the CPC leadership helps unify people's thinking and actions, and pool various resources and forces to form great synergy.

Second, the CPC principles of "serving the people and relying on the people" and "being realistic and pragmatic" provide guidance and a mechanism for the effective execution of relevant poverty alleviation policies.

Third, as more officials are mobilized to go to work in the countryside, state policies on poverty alleviation are better implemented at the grassroots level and reach eligible villagers, while the grassroots conditions are also reported to the decision-makers in a timely manner as reference for further improving relevant policies. This work experience at the front line also helps the officials in their own development.

Fourth, grassroots organizations are consolidated. Party branches are the driving forces propelling villagers, poor households in particular, to eliminate poverty and increase their incomes. They play the role of winning public support, pooling public wisdom, and valuing public efforts, maintaining close ties with the people, and enhancing villagers' understanding and support of Party and state policies, thus consolidating the CPC's governing status.

“最后一公里”

“最后一公里”原指完成长途跋涉的最后一段里程，被引申为完成一件事情最后的关键性步骤。长期以来，扶贫开发工作就受困于“最后一公里”的问题。

习近平在多个场合指出，要实施贫困村提升工程，培育壮大集体经济，完善基础设施，打通脱贫攻坚政策落实“最后一公里”。即把脱贫攻坚重点放在改善生产生活条件上，着重加强农田水利、交通通信等基础设施建设和技术培训、教育医疗等公共服务建设，特别是要解决好入村入户等“最后一公里”问题。支持贫困地区农民在本地或外出务工、创业，这是短期内增收最直接见效的办法。劳务输出地政府和输入地政府，对贫困人口外出务工要多想办法、多做实事。

为加强脱贫攻坚一线工作力量，中央要求，每个贫困村都要派驻村工作队，每个贫困户都要有帮扶责任人。截至2019年4月，全国累计选派300多万县级以上机关、国有企事业单位干部参加驻村帮扶，

The "Last-Mile" Problem

The "last-mile" problem refers to the last part of a journey. It is a metaphor to describe the last hurdle to clear before completing a task. China's poverty alleviation effort has been dogged by "last-mile" problems.

Xi Jinping has more than once talked about removing the last hurdle in implementing poverty elimination policies. By this he means improvement projects in poor villages, developing a collective economy, and improving local infrastructure. To be more specific, the focus is on improving rural living and production conditions, improving farmlands, irrigation, transportation and communications facilities, and providing technical training, education, medical services and other public services, particularly granting access to local villages and households.

Helping the rural population find jobs locally or elsewhere is a most effective way to increase their incomes within a short period of time. The governments of localities that are net importers or exporters of labor must take practical measures to facilitate employment for migrant workers.

To reinforce the frontline work of poverty elimination, the central authorities require that every poor village must have one resident working team and every poor household have one person assigned to help them. By April 2019, some 3 million officials had been

在岗的第一书记20.6万人、驻村干部70万人。他们积极帮助群众出主意干实事，推动扶贫政策措施落地落实，打通了精准扶贫“最后一公里”。

assigned to poverty alleviation missions. Of these, 206,000 were serving as on-post first Party secretaries, and 700,000 were resident working team members. These people have offered advice to the villagers and done solid work in the execution of poverty alleviation policies, thus solving the “last-mile” problems.

坚持精准方略，
提高脱贫实效

Employing Targeted Poverty Elimination to Achieve Anticipated Results

贫困地区

贫困地区是指那些贫困人口数量、贫困深重程度高于其他区域的地区。改革开放以来，中国大规模的扶贫开发行动以特定时期所确定的贫困地区为工作重点。1982年，国务院在甘肃的定西地区、河西地区和宁夏的西海固地区（简称“三西地区”)划定了28个重点扶持县。1984年,《中共中央 国务院关于帮助贫困地区尽快改变面貌的通知》发布，基本奠定了全国贫困地区大致范围。《通知》指出，由于自然条件、工作基础和政策落实情况的差异，农村经济还存在发展不平衡的状况，特别是还有几千万人口的地区仍未摆脱贫困，群众的温饱问题尚未完全解决。其中绝大部分是山区和边远地区，有的还是少数民族聚居地区和革命老根据地。解决贫困地区的问题要突出重点，特别是集中力量解决十几个连片贫困地区的问题。此后的扶贫开发工作虽对贫困地区的范围有所调整，但大体遵循了上述范围界定的基本思路。1986年，国务院在全国范围内

Impoverished Areas

"Impoverished areas" is how China defines areas with larger impoverished populations and greater poverty than other areas. At different stages since the late 1970s China has launched large-scale poverty alleviation programs targeting different impoverished areas.

For instance, in 1982, the State Council designated 28 poor counties in Gansu Province and Ningxia Hui Autonomous Region. In 1984, the central leadership issued a document entitled Notice on Helping the Impoverished Areas Improve Their Conditions, which delimited the general scope of poor areas across the country. The document pointed out that the imbalance in local natural conditions, economic development and implementation of policies resulted in imbalances in the rural economy, leaving millions of people still living in poverty with their basic needs not yet met. Most of the areas involved are mountainous or remote, and many are ethnic minority areas or old revolutionary bases. To tackle poverty, the focus should be on a dozen or so contiguous areas of extreme poverty.

Despite some adjustments over the following decades, the configuration of impoverished areas has remained more or less the same over the years.

In 1986, the State Council designated

陆续确定了331个国家重点扶持贫困县。1988年，国务院在河北、内蒙古、四川、甘肃、青海和新疆的牧区中又确定了27个国家重点扶持县。各省、自治区也根据各自具体情况确定了300多个省级重点扶持县。由此，到1988年年底，全国共有贫困县664个。后来个别省、自治区增加扶持范围，全国贫困县总数达到699个。1994年，列入《国家八七扶贫攻坚计划（1994—2000年）》扶持范围的贫困县调整为592个。2001年，根据《中国农村扶贫开发纲要（2001—2010年）》的要求，中国重新确定了592个国家扶贫开发工作重点县、14.8万个贫困村。

中共十八大以来，随着脱贫攻坚战的全面打响，贫困地区脱贫的重要性进一步凸显，被称为全面建成小康社会任务最繁重的区域，是打赢脱贫攻坚战的主战场。

331 key impoverished counties entitled to state assistance. Two years later in 1988, 27 more counties in Gansu, Hebei, Inner Mongolia, Qinghai, Sichuan and Xinjiang were added to the list. Provincial-level governments also designated more than 300 counties under their jurisdiction for special support. This raised the total number of poor counties to 664 by the end of 1988. A further expansion of the scope of assistance brought the number to 699 nationwide.

According to the Seven-year Program for Lifting 80 Million People Out of Poverty (1994-2000), released in 1994, there were 592 key counties entitled for state poverty alleviation assistance across China. The number remained at 592 in the Outline for Development-oriented Poverty Alleviation of China's Rural Areas (2001-2010), involving 148,000 poor villages.

The impoverished areas are the main battlefields in China's war against poverty, as they have the toughest problems to tackle in building a moderately prosperous society in all respects.

深度贫困地区

作为中国经济社会发展不充分、不均衡的产物，贫困问题本身亦存在贫困程度的差异，而深度贫困地区则是贫困地区中贫困程度深重，脱贫难度较大的区域。习近平指出，脱贫攻坚本来就是一场硬仗，而深度贫困地区脱贫攻坚是这场硬仗中的硬仗。

深度贫困地区主要是指以下三类地区：一是连片的深度贫困地区，如西藏和四省藏区、南疆四地州、四川凉山、云南怒江、甘肃临夏等地区，生存环境恶劣，致贫原因复杂，基础设施和公共服务缺口大，贫困发生率普遍在20%左右。二是深度贫困县，据国务院扶贫办对全国最困难的20%的贫困县所做的分析，贫困发生率

Severely Impoverished Areas

As a result of inadequate and unbalanced economic and social development, different areas in China face different levels of poverty. Severely impoverished areas are areas with extreme poverty and are the most difficult places to eliminate poverty. In the words of Xi Jinping, the fight against poverty is itself a tough one, and the fight in the severely impoverished areas is the toughest of all.

The severely impoverished areas in China include the following:

(1) Contiguous areas of extreme poverty: Tibet, the Tibetan ethnic areas in Sichuan, Yunnan, Gansu and Qinghai provinces, the four prefectures in southern Xinjiang (Hotan, Aksu, Kashi and the Kizilsu Kirgiz Autonomous Prefecture), and the three prefectures (Liangshan in Sichuan, Nujiang in Yunnan and Linxia in Gansu). These places suffer extremely poor living conditions; there are complex causes of poverty and a great shortage of infrastructure and public services, and the poverty headcount ratio remains at 20 percent;

(2) Counties suffering extreme poverty: According to an analysis of 20 percent of China's poorest counties conducted by the State Council Leading Group Office of Poverty Alleviation and Development,

平均在23%，县均贫困人口近3万人，分布在14个省区。三是贫困村，全国12.8万个建档立卡贫困村居住着60%的贫困人口，基础设施和公共服务严重滞后，村两委班子能力普遍不强，四分之三的村无合作经济组织，三分之二的村无集体经济，无人管事、无人干事、无钱办事现象突出。

these counties are scattered across 14 provinces and autonomous regions, and have an average poverty headcount ratio of 23 percent, each with an average of nearly 30,000 impoverished people; and

(3) Poor villages: There are 128,000 poor villages, where live 60 percent of China's poor population. Their infrastructure and public services lag far behind, and their Party branches and villagers' committees are very weak. Three quarters of these villages have no cooperatives and two-thirds have no collective economy. No one is responsible for village affairs, no one takes the initiative to do poverty alleviation work, and the villages have no money for projects.

“三区三州”

“三区三州”地区包含西藏、四省藏区、南疆四地州和四川省凉山彝族自治州、云南省怒江傈僳族自治州、甘肃省临夏回族自治州。这些地区不仅贫困发生率高、贫困程度深，而且基础条件薄弱、致贫原因复杂、发展严重滞后、公共服务不足，一直是集中力量攻克贫困的难中之难、坚中之坚。

随着脱贫攻坚深入推进，截至2019年年底，“三区三州”贫困人口减少到43万人，贫困发生率下降到2%。

The Most Impoverished Three Regions and Three Prefectures

The "three regions" are Tibet, the Tibetan ethnic areas of Sichuan, Yunnan, Gansu and Qinghai provinces, and the four prefectures in southern Xinjiang (Hotan, Aksu, Kashi and the Kizilsu Kirgiz Autonomous Prefecture). The "three prefectures" are Liangshan in Sichuan, Nujiang in Yunnan and Linxia in Gansu.

With a high incidence and high intensity of poverty, poor infrastructure, complex causes of poverty, backward development and lack of public services, these places have remained the toughest challenges in China's poverty alleviation campaign.

Thanks to the great efforts made, the three regions and three prefectures saw their impoverished population dropping to 430,000 and poverty headcount ratio to 2 percent by the end of 2019.

“直过民族”

“直过民族”是对生活在中国境内，在新中国成立前仍处于原始社会或奴隶社会，新中国成立后跨越几种社会形态，直接过渡到社会主义社会的少数民族的统称。“直过民族”是中国56个民族中的特殊成员，他们几乎“一夜之间”跨越了其他民族上千年的历程。

“直过民族”在不断跨越的进程中，其原始落后的面貌得到了巨大的改变，社会发展水平大幅度提高，生产方式、文化习俗、生活观念等也经历了激烈的碰撞和变革。同时，“直过民族”的历史局限性导致其在一定程度上对直接过渡和改革开放还不适应，这种不适应性在全面建成小康社会的过程中正逐渐得到缓解，但仍然是制约“直过民族”脱贫攻坚的最大因素。

"Ethnic Groups with Cross-Stage Development"

"Ethnic groups with cross-stage development" refer to the minority ethnic groups that remained in a primitive or slave society before 1949 and developed directly into a socialist society after the establishment of the People's Republic. Almost overnight, they crossed many historic stages and traveled a journey that might have taken other ethnic groups centuries.

During their leapfrog development, these ethnic groups have seen a significant transformation in their primitive conditions, significant enhancements to their social development, and dramatic changes in their working conditions, culture, customs and values. But their historic limitations have also prevented them from adapting to the direct transformation and to reform and opening up. This is the biggest obstacle to their poverty elimination, despite some progress during China's nationwide advance toward moderate prosperity.

贫困县

中国自20世纪80年代中期在全国范围内开展有组织、有计划、大规模扶贫开发以来，一个基本做法是将贫困面较大、贫困程度较深的县作为实施扶贫开发的基本组织单位。这是因为，县一级是中国基层行政建制中组织机构最全、公共管理职能最强的基层组织，是承上启下的最重要环节，离贫困村、贫困人口的距离最近，有利于开展有针对性的扶贫开发工作。此外，将贫困面较大、贫困程度较重的县作为扶贫开发的重点单位，有利于将较大比重的贫困人口纳入扶贫工作范围，集中力量进行扶持。

1986年国家第一次确定贫困县，并以县为单位，以1985年年人均收入低于150元和少数民族地区年人均纯收入低于200元为标准，确定了331个国家重点扶持贫困县。1994年颁布的《国家八七扶贫攻坚计划（1994—2000年）》第二次确定贫困县，将1992年全县农民人均纯收入低

Poor Counties

China began large-scale planned poverty alleviation and development campaigns in the mid-1980s. The general approach was to designate poor counties as the basic units to receive state support. This is because in China, counties are the grassroots administrative divisions with complete organizations and strong public management. They are a key link in China's administrative system which can effectively carry out targeted policies to help poor villages and poor people out of poverty.

Designating counties with large poor populations and severe poverty as the focus of development-oriented alleviation has brought these poor populations under the umbrella of national campaigns and concentrated the resources available to help them.

China designated poor counties for the first time in 1986. A total of 331 key counties whose per-capita income was below 150 yuan in 1985 were targeted for state assistance. The threshold in ethnic minority areas was below 200 yuan.

In 1994, the state renewed the list of poor counties in the Seven-year Program for Lifting 80 Million People Out of Poverty (1994-2000). Counties where farmers had a per-capita net income below 400 yuan in 1992 were designated as national-level poor

于400元的县全部纳入国家级贫困县，原来的贫困县高于700元的一律退出。这次调整确定了592个国家重点扶持贫困县。2001年国家颁布《中国农村扶贫开发纲要（2001—2010年）》对国家重点扶持贫困县再次进行调整，改称国家扶贫开发工作重点县，总体规模仍保持592个。

2011年《中国农村扶贫开发纲要（2011—2020年）》确定14个集中连片特殊困难地区（简称连片特困地区）作为扶贫攻坚主战场，覆盖680个重点县。这些县加上没有在片区范围的国家扶贫开发工作重点县共832个，统称“贫困县”。国家确定2020年贫困县全部摘帽的就是这832个县。

counties entitled to state support, and those previously listed as "poor" were removed from the list if farmers there had a per-capita net income higher than 700 yuan. In total, 592 counties across China were listed as targets for national poverty alleviation.

In 2001, the state released the Outline for Development-oriented Poverty Alleviation of China's Rural Areas (2001-2010), and adjusted the list of key counties for poverty alleviation. The total number remained 592.

In 2011, the renewed Outline for Development-oriented Poverty Alleviation of China's Rural Areas (2011-2020) defined 14 contiguous areas of extreme poverty as the main battlefields against poverty, covering 680 key counties. Together with other poor counties located elsewhere, a total of 832 counties were designated as "key poor" ones where poverty must be eliminated by the year 2020.

贫困村

进入21世纪，随着《国家八七扶贫攻坚计划（1994—2000年）》完成，中国贫困人口集中连片的状况明显改变，贫困人口分布呈现出“大分散、小集中”的新特点，贫困人口主要集中聚居在那些地域偏远、交通不便、经济和社会事业发展相对滞后的村落。针对这一新的减贫形势，中国开始将贫困村作为扶贫开发的瞄准单元。中共十八大以来，精准扶贫精准脱贫成为打赢脱贫攻坚战的基本方略。准确找出贫困村在哪里、确定谁是贫困户，给他们建档立卡，成为精准扶贫的“一号工程”。为此，国务院扶贫办2014年4月印发《扶贫开发建档立卡工作方案》，明确了贫困村标准。贫困村识别原则上按照“一高一低一无”的标准进行，即行政村贫困发生率比全省贫困发生率高一倍以上，行政村2013年全村农民人均纯收入低于全省平均水平的60%，行政村无集体经济收入。2014年4月至10月，全国共识别出12.8万个贫困村、2948万贫困户、8962万贫困人口，基本摸清了全国贫困人口分布、致

Poor Villages

With the completion of the Seven-year Program for Lifting 80 Million People Out of Poverty (1994-2000), the conditions of contiguous poor areas had been notably improved. The remaining poor mainly lived in remote villages with poor transportation and backward economic and social development. To address this problem, China had turned to targeting poor villages as the focus of poverty reduction.

Since 2012, targeted poverty alleviation and elimination have been the overall strategy, so it is essential to determine which villages and households are eligible for state assistance. To this end, the State Council Leading Group Office of Poverty Alleviation and Development in 2014 released a Plan for Poverty Alleviation Registration, defining the standards for poor villages. Technically, a village would be labeled as "poor" if its poverty headcount ratio was more than double that of its province, if its per-capita net income was lower than 60 percent of the provincial average in 2013, and if the village had no collective economic earnings.

From April to October 2014, a total of 128,000 poor villages with 29.48 million poor households and 89.62 million impoverished people were identified. The government also gained a clear picture of their locations, the causes of their poverty, and their particular

贫原因、脱贫需求等“贫困家底”，建立起了全国统一的扶贫开发信息系统，为精准扶贫提供了大数据支撑。

needs for poverty elimination. A nationwide unified information system of poverty alleviation was thus created to provide big data for relevant endeavors.

贫困户

贫困户可简单理解为需要扶贫的家庭。然而，由于权力、信息等多种因素的影响，如何识别和确定贫困户成为有效减贫的前提条件。中共十八大以来，以精准扶贫为基本方略，中国的贫困户识别体制机制有了巨大的创新，达到了极高的贫困识别率，为脱贫攻坚奠定了重要基础。2014年国务院印发的《扶贫开发建档立卡工作方案》指出，贫困户识别要以农户收入为基本依据，综合考虑住房、教育、健康等情况，通过农户申请、民主评议、公示公告和逐级审核的方式，整户识别。由于农户收入精准测算比较困难，各地在自下而上的贫困识别上也探索了一些创新做法。如贵州省威宁县迤那镇五星村精准识别“四看工作法”，即“一看房，二看粮，三看劳动能力强不强，四看家中有没有读书郎”。每“一看”都有子指标并赋予相应分值。在民主评议中，由村民代表对申请农户按照“四看”法进行打分，再根据农户分值情况，从高往低排序识别出贫困农户。

Poor Households

Poor households are those that need assistance to get rid of poverty. To identify and determine which households are poor is a precondition for effective poverty reduction.

Since 2012, China has followed the strategy of targeted poverty alleviation and established a mechanism to identify poor households, thus laying a good foundation for poverty elimination.

According to the Plan for Poverty Alleviation Registration, issued by the State Council in 2014, the designation is based on household income, with due consideration given to housing, education and health conditions. Individual household applications will go through democratic appraisal, public notice and review by the authorities at each higher level, before a final ruling is made.

Since it is not easy to calculate the accurate income of individual households, different localities have created their own mechanisms to determine the true conditions. In Wuxing Village in Weining County, Guizhou Province, for example, the financial conditions of the household applicants are decided based on their housing and grain output, their ability to work, and whether they have school-age children. The villager representatives will rate these four items in a democratic appraisal, and the final scores are listed from the highest down so that the poorest households can be easily identified.

整村推进

进入21世纪，中国农村贫困人口分布呈现新的特征，由原来的以区域、县为单位集中分布，变为以村为单位集中分布。这就要求扶贫开发工作必须重心下移，工作到村，瞄准到户。只有这样，才能把扶贫开发的各项措施真正落到实处，尽快解决最贫困人口的温饱问题。为适应新的变化和要求，各地在实践中逐步摸索出整村推进扶贫开发的方式。

整村推进扶贫开发的内涵是以贫困村为基本单元，以贫困人口为对象，以村级扶贫规划为依据，以村级经济、社会、文化协调发展为目标，以改善基础条件、促进产业发展、加强能力建设、规范民主管理、树立文明新风、整治村容村貌、稳定解决温饱为主要内容的扶贫开发工作措施。

Village-Based Poverty Alleviation

As China entered the 21st century, its impoverished rural population showed newly featured distribution. Previously poor people were generally scattered across large regions or counties; now the scope had shrunk to villages. This required poverty alleviation work to focus on individual villages and households, so as to ensure that relevant policies be carried out in earnest to satisfy those most in need. Village-based development-oriented poverty alleviation was thus shaped and has proved effective across the country.

Poor villages now have their own poverty alleviation plans to encourage economic and cultural progress, improve infrastructure and the living environment, boost business development, provide greater skills, regulate democratic management, foster sound morals and values, and ensure that villagers have adequate food and clothing.

十八洞村

十八洞村位于湖南省花垣县排碧乡西南部，是一个纯苗族村寨。这里山高林密、民风淳朴、风景独特，因十八溶洞群得名。全村总面积14162亩，225户，939人，但耕地面积仅有817亩（全村人均耕地仅有0.83亩），2013年人均纯收入仅有1668元。因为贫困，村里不少年轻人成家也成了难题。2013年11月3日，习近平来到十八洞村调研，提出了“实事求是、因地制宜、分类指导、精准扶贫”十六字方针，并明确提出了“可复制”“可推广”的原则。

2018年，十八洞村修通了村里出山的路，村民的庭院也实现了通水改厕、架电亮灯；年产的300吨果子顺利拿到了有机食品认证和出口果园认证，每户村民分红不低于5000元；银行开到了村里，家门口也有了ATM机；村里矿泉水厂正式投产，

Shibadong Village

Shibadong is a village of the Miao people, located in Huayuan County, Hunan Province. Its name (literally "18 caves") comes from the 18 karst caves nearby. Despite the beautiful scenery they enjoy, the 225 households and 939 villagers share only 817 *mu* (54 hectares) of arable land, which means 0.83 *mu* for each villager. The village produced a per-capita net income of only 1,668 yuan in 2013. Poverty made it difficult for young village men to find wives, as few women would want to marry into this poor village.

The situation changed with the arrival of Xi Jinping, who visited Shibadong on an inspection tour on November 3, 2013. Xi proposed a principle for poverty alleviation: targeted efforts based on local conditions, and he also required that the approach be applicable to other locations.

Thanks to targeted development measures and assistance from all sides, great changes have taken place in Shibadong. The village now has tapped water, power access, indoor flushing toilets and a bank branch with an ATM. There are quality roads leading to the outside world. The village plantation, with a yearly yield of 300 tons of fruits, has obtained an organic certification for export, from which each household will earn a dividend of at least 5,000 yuan per year. A

十八个大溶洞景区也将开业；十八洞村村民的人均纯收入从1600多元增加到1万元以上，精准识别的533人全部脱贫摘帽。

mineral water plant has begun operation, and an 18-karst-cave tourist zone is to open soon. The per-capita net income has risen from a little more than 1,600 yuan to more than 10,000 yuan, and the 533 poor villagers no longer live in poverty.

补短板

习近平指出，中国经济社会发展的主要矛盾在新时代发生了变化，需要新的发展方略。当前中国经济社会发展的战略目标是全面建成小康社会，战略重点在于补齐短板，扶贫工作则是其中最薄弱的领域。

“补短板”思维是理解习近平扶贫工作思维方法的一个关键。早在2004年时，时任浙江省委书记的习近平就在省域层面提出“补短板”的思维方法：“全面建成小康社会，强调的不仅是‘小康’，而且更重要也更难做到的是‘全面’。‘小康’讲的是发展水平，‘全面’讲的是发展的平衡性、协调性、可持续性。”

“补短板”的发展战略是对马克思主义基本立场的坚守，同样也是对中国特色社会主义的创新和发展。习近平指出，“小康不小康，关键看老乡”，“在发展中补齐民生短

Improving Areas of Weakness

As the principal issues influencing China's economic and social development have changed in the new era, Xi Jinping points out that the country needs a new strategy for development. To fulfill the strategic goal of building a moderately prosperous society in all respects, the strategic focus should be on improving areas of weakness, of which poverty alleviation is the weakest link.

Xi made a similar proposal for Zhejiang Province in 2004 when he was secretary of its provincial CPC committee. To build a moderately prosperous society in all respects, the focus should be equally on "a moderately prosperous society" and "in all respects" – the latter being more important and more difficult to achieve. "A moderately prosperous society" represents a certain level of development, while "in all respects" extends that level of development to one that is balanced, coordinated and sustainable.

The idea of improving areas of weakness reflects a Marxist stance and contribution to the theory of socialism with Chinese characteristics. Xi Jinping's vision on development and moderate prosperity is like this: Whether China has achieved prosperity will be judged by the conditions of

板、促进社会公平正义”，体现了他对于什么是发展，什么是小康社会的深刻思考。

the rural areas, and China will improve the weak links related to people's wellbeing and enhance social fairness and justice through development.

问题导向

增强问题意识，强化问题导向，进而形成解决问题的新体制新机制，是中共十八大以来以习近平同志为核心的党中央治国理政的重要思想方法和工作方法。

在扶贫工作中，问题导向主要体现为“坚持从严要求，促进真抓实干”，即及时解决脱贫攻坚中影响脱贫攻坚进程的各类态度、做法、方法问题。对此，习近平指出，要坚持问题导向，集中力量解决脱贫领域“四个意识”不强、责任落实不到位、工作措施不精准、资金管理使用不规范、工作作风不扎实、考核评估不严格等突出问题。要认真总结，完善考核工作机制，坚持问题导向，敢于较真碰硬，使考核工作更加科学有效、符合实际，进而有力督促引导各地区做到精准扶贫、精准脱贫，不断提高脱贫攻坚工作成效。

2018年5月31日，中共中央政治局召开会议审议《关于打赢脱贫攻坚战三年行动的指导意见》，明确提出突出问题导向，优化政策供给，下足绣花功夫，着力激发贫困人口内生动力，夯实贫困人口稳定脱贫基础等具体要求。这意味着各地在扶贫

Problem-Oriented Approaches

Having a strong awareness of problems, taking problem-oriented approaches, then forming new mechanisms for solving the problems – this has been a major tactic in governance by the CPC Central Committee with Xi Jinping at its core since 2012.

In poverty alleviation, taking problem-oriented approaches means setting strict requirements, doing solid work, and finding timely solutions to problems related to attitudes, conduct and methods. Xi insists on tackling such problems as weakness in the "Four Consciousnesses," failure in taking on responsibility, not being down-to-earth in daily work, imposing irrelevant measures, irregularities in fund management and usage, and lax review and evaluation. The evaluation mechanism is being improved, with thorough methods and determined action to crack hard nuts, in order to ensure that evaluation is effective and pragmatic and can truly guide targeted poverty alleviation.

On May 31, 2018, the Political Bureau of the CPC Central Committee met to deliberate a Three-year Guideline on Winning the Battle Against Poverty. The document proposed taking problem-oriented approaches, improving relevant policies, doing meticulous work, fostering the internal initiative of the

工作中，需要认真反思以往“资金+盖房”的单一做法，集中力量改善深度贫困地区发展条件，着力解决深度贫困地区群众特殊困难，树立脱贫光荣导向，弘扬自尊、自爱、自强精神，提高贫困群众的自我发展能力。

在脱贫攻坚中坚持问题导向，既是实现精准扶贫精准脱贫的现实需要，也是将从严治党要求贯穿于脱贫攻坚全过程的重要保障。即，只有实施最严格的考核评估才能保证脱贫过程扎实、脱贫结果真实，只有优良的工作作风才能保障脱贫攻坚有力有序不断推进。总之，唯有坚持问题导向，方能确保打赢脱贫攻坚战，确保到2020年贫困地区和贫困人口同全国一道进入全面小康社会。

poor, and laying sound foundations for them to escape poverty. With these requirements, officials need to reflect upon their previous practice of "simply providing money and building housing." They should instead concentrate the resources to boost the development of deeply impoverished areas, help the severely impoverished solve their special problems, foster their pride in getting rid of poverty, and enhance their capacity for self-development.

Problem-oriented approaches are needed in practical work. Strict review and evaluation can prompt effective work and true delivery, and proper conduct on the part of officials can result in constant and orderly progress in poverty elimination. This will ensure victory in the battle against poverty, with all poor regions and disadvantaged people entering a moderately prosperous society by 2020 together with the rest of the country.

精准扶贫

精准扶贫是中国贫困治理的重大理论创新，是中共中央治国理政新理念新思想新战略的重要组成部分。中共十八大以来，基于习近平关于精准扶贫的一系列重要论述，中国共产党治理贫困工作翻开新篇章：脱贫攻坚战在全国全面打响，国家贫困治理体系日渐完善，减贫实践取得历史最好成绩。从政策设计层面来看，精准扶贫有着明确的减贫目标，是问题导向的贫困治理创新，是提高中国减贫成效的策略性选择。从新时代中国特色社会主义的背景以及习近平有关扶贫工作重要论述的整体来看，精准扶贫不仅是减贫事业的创新，更是治国理政思想的重要发展。

这种创新性的贫困治理理念及严谨的政策体系，使得脱贫攻坚取得了亮眼的减贫成绩，并对中国经济社会发展产生了诸多积极而深远的影响，充分显示了其实践价值。在贫困治理方面，精准扶贫不仅破解了贫困治理固有的若干难题，而且提升了扶贫开发的效能；在经济社会发展方面，精准扶贫一方面激活了农村基层社会治理，另一方面促进了区域经济社会的整

Targeted Poverty Alleviation

Targeted poverty alleviation is one of China's greatest theoretical innovations. It is an important component of the central leadership's philosophy of governance.

Since the 18th CPC National Congress in 2012, the CPC has written a new chapter in its fight against poverty in accordance with a series of views and proposals put forward by Xi Jinping. A nationwide battle against poverty has been launched, a system for poverty alleviation has been improved, and the country has achieved the best-ever results in poverty reduction.

China's targeted poverty alleviation is an innovation in poverty governance with a problem-oriented approach and clear goals for poverty reduction. It is a major development in China's governance philosophy and the right approach to ensure success.

Guided by a creative philosophy and precise policies, China has made outstanding progress in poverty elimination. This has exerted a positive and far-reaching influence on its economic and social development that fully demonstrates the practical value of the strategy.

Targeted poverty alleviation has tackled many tough problems in poverty, and increased the impact of development-oriented poverty

体发展。此外，精准扶贫还在激活基层农村社会治理、提升扶贫资源配置的公正性等方面产生了积极影响。

脱贫攻坚彰显了中国特色减贫之路的新发展，精准扶贫方略包含了反贫困的中国智慧与中国方案，对于中国打赢脱贫攻坚战以及完善贫困治理体系具有非凡的意义。同时，作为科学的理论创新，其对于国际减贫事业同样具有重要的启示意义。

alleviation. It inspires local management of rural communities and promotes regional development as a whole. It also promotes justice in the allocation of poverty-alleviation resources.

China's creative philosophy and unique approaches are key to its own poverty reduction; they also offer invaluable experience to international poverty reduction endeavors.

"四个问题"

以精准扶贫方略来实现"两不愁三保障"，消除绝对贫困，这相对于此前的贫困治理体系而言，不啻是一个难题，不仅需要加大资源的投入力度，而且需要在扶贫实践技术层面进行创新。首先，精准扶贫作为一项自上而下推行的社会政策，其本身就面临科层结构造成政策走样的风险。其次，在目前由且只能由政府主导的贫困治理体制下，贫困人群多元化的减贫需求亦面临"政府失灵"的困境。再次，由于层级治理信息不对称等问题的客观存在，地方政府、扶贫对象等的机会主义行为也难以避免。这些都构成了"精准"的客观障碍。在具体实践中，这些难题集中体现为"扶持谁、谁来扶、怎么扶、如何退"四个问题。以习近平扶贫论述为根本遵循，脱贫攻坚系统性地破解了这四个问题在实践中面临的各种障碍。

具体而言，解决好"扶持谁"问题，要坚持精准扶贫、精准脱贫，逐村逐户开展贫困识别，对识别出的贫困村、贫困户建档立卡，通过"回头看"和甄别调整，不断提高识别准确率。解决好"谁来扶"

Four Key Issues in Poverty Alleviation

To guarantee that the people have their basic living needs and access to compulsory education, basic medical services and safe housing, and to eliminate absolute poverty, through targeted alleviation measures – this is a great challenge, as great inputs of resources and creative measures and mechanisms are required.

First, this top-down social policy might not be carried out to the letter due to the administrative hierarchy. Second, under the current government-dominated poverty governance system, the diverse needs of the impoverished people may face problems of "government failure." Third, due to the asymmetric information in hierarchy management, opportunist actions by local governments and the recipients of aid are unavoidable. All these pose objective obstacles to "targeted" assistance.

In practice, these obstacles often emerge as "four key issues in poverty alleviation" – who needs help, who provides help, how to help, and how to be removed from the poverty list.

To be specific, to find out "who needs help," it is necessary to identify and register poor villages and poor households, with timely adjustment through follow-up checks

问题，关键在于责任落实到人。全国累计选派300多万县级以上机关、国有企事业单位干部参加驻村帮扶，一线扶贫力量明显加强，打通了精准扶贫“最后一公里”。解决好“怎么扶”问题，要实施“五个一批”工程，即发展生产脱贫一批、易地搬迁脱贫一批、生态补偿脱贫一批、发展教育脱贫一批、社会保障兜底一批，开对“药方子”，拔掉“穷根子”。解决好“如何退”问题，一是设定时间表，实现贫困县有序退出；二是留出缓冲期，在一定时间内实行摘帽不摘政策；三是实行严格评估，按照摘帽标准验收；四是实行逐户销号，做到脱贫到人。

for accuracy.

To determine "who provides help," responsibilities have to be specified. Over three million officials have been dispatched to poor villages to reinforce the front line.

To answer the question of "how to help," five targeted measures are employed according to local conditions: boosting the economy to create more jobs for the disadvantaged, relocating those living under adverse natural conditions, providing eco-jobs for impoverished people, improving education in poor areas, and improving social security for poverty elimination.

As to the question of "how to be removed from the poverty list," a timetable has been set for the poor counties to be removed from the poverty list; there will be a grace period when they can continue to enjoy relevant preferential policies; strict evaluation will be conducted in line with relevant standards; and each person and each household will be removed from the poverty list only if they meet these standards.

建档立卡

建档立卡，是指在全国范围内建立贫困户、贫困村、贫困县和连片特困地区电子信息档案，向贫困户发放《扶贫手册》，并以此构建全国扶贫信息网络系统，为精准扶贫工作奠定基础。2014年以来，全国扶贫系统开展了贫困识别建档立卡工作，建档立卡对象包括贫困户、贫困村、贫困县和连片特困地区。国务院有关部门通过在全国范围逐村逐户开展贫困识别，共识别出12.8万个贫困村，2948万贫困户、8962万贫困人口，基本摸清了全国贫困人口分布、致贫原因、脱贫需求等信息，建立起了全国统一的扶贫开发信息系统。经过2015至2018年的动态调整，进一步完善建档立卡贫困识别信息数据库和帮扶台账。通过建档立卡，有关单位可以对贫困户和贫困村进行精准识别，了解贫困状况，分析致贫原因，摸清帮扶需求，明确帮扶主体，落实帮扶措施，开展考核问效，实施动态管理。同时，建档立卡也有利于对贫困县和连片特困地区进行监测和评估，分析掌握扶贫开发工作情况，为扶贫开发决策和考核提供依据。

Poverty Registration

Poverty registration refers to the filing of electronic information about poor households, villages, counties and contiguous areas of extreme poverty across the country, before a poverty alleviation handbook is distributed to each eligible household. Based on this, a nationwide poverty alleviation information network is being built.

In 2014, a total of 128,000 poor villages with 29.48 million poor households and 89.62 million impoverished people were identified and registered. The government also obtained a general picture of their locations, the causes of their poverty, and their particular needs for poverty elimination. A nationwide unified information system of poverty alleviation was thus built to provide big data for relevant endeavors.

With timely adjustment between 2015 and 2018, the poverty identification and registration databank and assistance account books were further improved. Relevant units can obtain detailed information about the recipients of assistance – the causes of their poverty and their individual needs – and carry out targeted measures to help them and review the results. Likewise, the authorities can better monitor and evaluate progress in poor counties and contiguous areas, and take these as a source of reference for decision-making and performance review.

大数据时代的扶贫开发，需要搭建一个人人可关注、人人可参与的公众扶贫参与平台，而这些都要依据权威、准确和透明的数据。可以说，建档立卡是新时期扶贫开发工作的一个“破冰工程”。

Poverty alleviation in the big data era requires that a platform be available for the public to learn about and participate in assistance programs, on top of which authoritative, accurate and transparent data are essential. Poverty registration is an ice-breaker in this regard.

"回头看"

一是建档立卡"回头看"。2013年年底中共中央办公厅、国务院办公厅印发《关于创新机制扎实推进农村扶贫开发工作的意见》，要求国家制定统一的扶贫对象识别办法，对每个贫困村、贫困户建档立卡，建设全国扶贫信息网络系统。从2014年起，国务院扶贫办统筹顶层设计，按照"一年打基础、两年完善、三年规范运行"的总体思路，制定《扶贫开发建档立卡工作方案》和《扶贫开发建档立卡指标体系》，明确了全国统一的建档立卡标准和程序。2015年8月至2016年6月，全国动员近200万人开展建档立卡"回头看"，通过对2014年建档立卡数据进行重新比对，补录贫困人口807万人，剔除识别不准人口929万人，扶贫识别的精准度进一步提高。

二是脱贫人口"回头看"。国务院扶贫办自2019年起，对所有已经脱贫的贫困人口适时开展"回头看"，看每一个脱贫家庭是否真正脱贫，还存在哪些返贫风险，并针对每个贫困家庭不同的困难和问题，采取对应的措施。

Follow-Up Checks

First, follow-up checks of poverty registration. In late 2013, the central authorities issued the Decision on Creating New Mechanisms for Promoting Rural Poverty Alleviation and Development, devising methods to identify impoverished targets, having every poor village and household registered, and building a nationwide unified information system of poverty alleviation.

In 2014, the State Council Leading Group Office of Poverty Alleviation and Development issued the Plan for Poverty Alleviation Registration and the Index System for Poverty Alleviation Registration. The two documents set national unified standards and procedures for poverty registration.

From August 2015 to June 2016, follow-up checks were made of the 2014 registration information, which identified 8.07 million additional impoverished people and removed 9.29 million false ones from the register, thus making the information more accurate.

Second, follow-up checks on poverty elimination. Starting in 2019, the Leading Group Office of Poverty Alleviation and Development has conducted such follow-up checks to make sure that every household has really escaped poverty and faces no danger of slipping back into poverty. Through follow-up checks, corresponding measures will be taken targeting the problems and difficulties every family encounters.

“五个一批”

习近平强调，解决好“怎么扶”的问题，需要按照贫困地区和贫困人口的具体情况，实施“五个一批”工程。一是发展生产脱贫一批：引导和支持所有有劳动能力的人立足当地资源，实现就地脱贫，依靠自己的双手开创美好明天。二是易地搬迁脱贫一批：贫困人口很难实现就地脱贫的要实施易地搬迁，按规划、分年度、有计划组织实施，确保搬得出、稳得住、能致富。三是生态补偿脱贫一批：加大贫困地区生态保护修复力度，增加重点生态功能区转移支付，扩大政策实施范围，让有劳动能力的贫困人口就地转成护林员等生态保护人员。四是发展教育脱贫一批：治贫先治愚，扶贫先扶智，国家教育经费要继续向贫困地区倾斜、向基础教育倾斜、

Five Measures for Poverty Elimination

Regarding the question of "how to help," Xi Jinping has proposed five measures to be taken according to the specific conditions of poverty-stricken areas and impoverished populations:

(1) Boosting the economy to create more jobs for the disadvantaged. All those with the ability to work should be guided and encouraged to work for a better future with their own hands and rely on local resources to end poverty;

(2) Relocating those living under adverse natural conditions. Those who cannot escape poverty locally can be relocated in a planned and organized way. Efforts are needed to ensure smooth relocation and settlement, and ensure those involved have the means to better themselves;

(3) Providing eco-jobs for the poor. China has strengthened eco-environmental restoration and protection in impoverished areas, increased transfer payments in important ecological areas, expanded the scope of those eligible for preferential policies, and granted poor people with the ability to work the opportunity to serve as forest rangers or do other eco-work;

(4) Improving education in poor areas. The best way to help the poor is to raise their

向职业教育倾斜，帮助贫困地区改善办学条件，对农村贫困家庭幼儿特别是留守儿童给予特殊关爱。五是社会保障兜底一批：对贫困人口中完全或部分丧失劳动能力的人，由社会保障来兜底，统筹协调农村扶贫标准和农村低保标准，加大其他形式的社会救助力度；通过加强医疗保险和医疗救助，使新型农村合作医疗和大病保险政策对贫困人口倾斜；同时，也应高度重视革命老区脱贫攻坚工作。

“五个一批”的减贫思想，为具有差异的贫困人群提供了不同的发展模式，避免了单一减贫手段在面对不同贫困群体时的局限性。通过精准施策、精准扶贫，既充分满足了基本需求，又为贫困人口福利水平的提升营造了发展机会。

educational level. National education funds will continue to be weighted toward poverty-stricken areas, for basic education and vocational education. The education services in impoverished areas will be improved, and due attention be given to young children from impoverished rural households, especially "left-behind" children who stay in rural areas while their parents are away working as migrant workers; and

(5) Improving social security for poverty alleviation. Among the poverty-stricken population, those who have completely or partially lost the ability to work will be guaranteed social security. The standard of rural poverty alleviation allowance and that of rural subsistence allowance will be readjusted, and other forms of social aid be provided. Medical insurance and medical aid will be increased for poverty relief, and the rural poor will be covered by the new rural cooperative medical insurance and the serious illness insurance. More poverty relief efforts will be made to support the old revolutionary base areas of the CPC before the founding of the PRC.

These five measures offer different models of development for disadvantaged people living under different conditions on the one hand, and overcome the limitations any single method may have on the other. While satisfying the people's basic needs, they also offer opportunities of better quality of life.

“六个精准”

2015年6月，习近平在贵州考察时提出了扶贫开发工作“六个精准”的基本要求，即扶持对象精准、项目安排精准、资金使用精准、措施到户精准、因村派人（第一书记）精准、脱贫成效精准。“六个精准”涵盖了贫困治理的基本方面，为扶贫政策设计与地方治理创新提供了基本依据。

“六个精准”不仅强调贫困治理对象、项目和目标等的精准，同时也注重实现彼此之间的匹配。只有把真正的贫困人口弄清楚，才能做到真扶贫、扶真贫；只有明确了各级政府责任，责任落实到人，才能做到扶贫项目优先安排、扶贫资金优先保障；只有按照贫困地区和贫困人口的具体

Six Elements of Targeted Poverty Alleviation

Xi Jinping talked about six elements of targeted poverty alleviation during his inspection tour of Guizhou Province in June 2015:

(1) Institutional innovations are needed to ensure that the recipients are those in need;

(2) The projects are adapted to the eligible recipients;

(3) The funds are effectively used;

(4) Appropriate measures are taken for individual households;

(5) Capable workers (first Party branch secretary) are dispatched to individual villages; and

(6) The results of poverty alleviation reach expectations.

These instructions cover the fundamentals of poverty governance and guide policy making and local management innovation. The six elements above are mutually relevant:

- Only with accurate information about the true poor populations can targeted assistance reach the households in need;
- Only with clear responsibilities defined for governments and officials can priority be given to projects and funds

情况施策，才能在各地千差万别的情况下因地制宜实现脱贫目标。

for poverty relief purposes; and

- Only with targeted policies being tailored for poor areas and poor populations can effective poverty alleviation be attained for different local conditions.

“七个强化”

2017年2月21日，中共中央政治局就国家脱贫攻坚形势和更好实施精准扶贫进行第三十九次集体学习。习近平在主持学习时强调，言必信，行必果。农村贫困人口如期脱贫、贫困县全部摘帽、解决区域性整体贫困，是全面建成小康社会的底线任务，是中国共产党作出的庄严承诺。为此，必须强化领导责任、强化资金投入、强化部门协同、强化东西协作、强化社会合力、强化基层活力、强化任务落实。通过做好这“七个强化”，集中力量攻坚克难，更好推进精准扶贫、精准脱贫，确保如期实现脱贫攻坚目标。

从中国扶贫开发的长时段来看，“七个强化”是对中国过去扶贫经验——“加强领导是根本、把握精准是要义、增加投入是保障、各方参与是合力、群众参与是基础”——的继承和发展。从脱贫攻坚的实

Seven Aspects of Reinforcing Poverty Alleviation Work

On February 21, 2017, the Political Bureau of the CPC Central Committee had its 39th group study session, with the subject being poverty elimination. Xi Jinping chaired the session and reiterated that promises must be kept. To help the rural population eliminate poverty as scheduled, lift all poor counties out of poverty and solve overall regional poverty are the CPC's promise to build a moderately prosperous society in all respects.

To honor this promise, efforts are needed to:

(1) reinforce the leadership's sense of responsibility;

(2) increase funds;

(3) facilitate coordination among government departments;

(4) enhance cooperation between the east and the west;

(5) build social synergy;

(6) restore the vigor of communities; and

(7) ensure that tasks are completed.

These are a continuation of the past experience in fighting poverty: There must be effective leadership, targeted efforts, adequate inputs, and wide participation and contribution.

With all these efforts, China can

践来看，“七个强化”从整体入手，强调以战略思维谋全局，以系统思维聚合力，为更好实施精准扶贫、打赢脱贫攻坚战提供了重要的方法论指导，指明了在扶贫领域推进国家贫困治理体系和治理能力现代化的基本路径。

concentrate its resources on challenging issues, better advance its targeted poverty elimination campaign, and meet its goals as planned. This will also help modernize state governance.

因地制宜

“因地制宜”的基本意思是指根据各地的具体情况，制定适宜的办法，其较好概括了精准扶贫精准脱贫的基本要求，与“因人因户因村施策”共同构成了精准扶贫的核心要义。这一概念屡见习近平关于精准扶贫的论述中，例如，“因地制宜、因村因户因人施策的帮扶体系”“市县抓落实，就是要因地制宜，从当地实际出发，推动脱贫攻坚各项政策措施落地生根”“帮扶措施一定要实，因地制宜、因人因户施策，找准症结把准脉，开对药方拔‘穷根’”。

习近平以河北省阜平县为例，生动阐释了“因地制宜”的含义：推进扶贫开发、推动经济社会发展，首先要有一个好思路、好路子。要坚持从实际出发，因地制宜，理清思路、完善规划、找准突破口。比如，阜平有300多万亩山场，森林覆盖率、植被覆盖率比较高，适合发展林果

Acting According to Local Conditions

To act according to local conditions means devising appropriate measures suited to local realities. This is a basic lesson of China's targeted poverty alleviation. To make it specific, targeted measures are tailored for each village, each household and each individual in severely poverty-stricken areas.

Xi Jinping has emphasized this point on different occasions. He demands that cities and counties be responsible for the execution of relevant policies according to local conditions, and make sure that these policies will take root and bear fruit. He likens targeted measures to "feeling the pulse of a patient" and "issuing the right prescription" by a doctor of traditional Chinese medicine.

He takes Fuping County in Hebei Province as an example. There must be good ideas and well-designed approaches that are applicable to local realities. With good planning, it is easy to make breakthroughs at the right point.

For instance, Fuping County has 3 million *mu* (200,000 hectares) of mountainous land, with a high forest coverage rate, which is suitable for orchards, plantations, and animal husbandry. There is a group of waterfalls and a museum in the old revolutionary base area. These are good tourist resources to develop,

业、种植业、畜牧业。还有晋察冀边区革命纪念馆和天生桥瀑布群这样的景区，离北京、天津这样的大城市都不算远，又北靠五台山、南临西柏坡，发展旅游业大有潜力。要做到宜农则农、宜林则林、宜牧则牧、宜开发生态旅游则搞生态旅游，真正把自身比较优势发挥好，使贫困地区发展扎实建立在自身有利条件的基础之上。

given the county's proximity to Beijing and Tianjin, the Buddhist resort of Wutai Mountain, and Xibaipo (location of the CPC's headquarters before it moved to Beiping, now Beijing, in March 1949).

Xi points out that different localities should make good use of their own comparative strengths to develop either agriculture, forestry, animal husbandry or eco-tourism, whatever is most suitable to them, so as to lay a solid foundation for long-term development.

因户施策

脱贫攻坚贵在精准，重在精准。要在精准施策上出实招，在精准推进上下实功，在精准落地上见实效。解决好“扶持谁”的问题，就是确保把真正的贫困人口弄清楚，把贫困程度、致贫原因等搞清楚，找对“穷根”、明确靶向，做到扶真贫、真扶贫，做到因户施策、因人施策。解决好“谁来扶”的问题，就是坚持中央统筹、省负总责、市县抓落实的工作机制，强化党政一把手负总责的责任制，坚持大扶贫格局，健全东西部协作和党政机关、部队、人民团体、国有企业定点扶贫机制，做到分工明确、责任清晰、任务到人、考核到位。

Targeted Measures for Each Household

"Targeted" is the core nature of all the measures designed for poverty elimination and their implementation. Real efforts are needed in targeted policy-making and in delivering real results in policy implementation.

Regarding the question of "who needs help," accurate information is to be obtained about the poor, their conditions and the root causes of their problems, so that targeted policies can be tailored for different households and individuals in need.

Regarding the question of "who provides help," the working mechanism will continue whereby the central leadership makes overall plans, provincial authorities take overall responsibility, and city and county authorities take charge of implementation. Top Party and government officials at each level are responsible for poverty alleviation under their jurisdiction. All resources will be integrated to build synergy, and the mechanism be improved to enhance the cooperation between the east and the west, with a clear division of labor and responsibilities among Party and government departments, the military, people's organizations, and state-owned enterprises, with specific tasks for their staff assigned to poverty alleviation, and with effective evaluation of their performance.

在地区差异性的基础上，习近平进一步指出，现在已经不搞大片区扶贫了，不是整个西北、整个东北怎么扶的问题，而是在不同区域里碎片化的情况下怎么抓的问题。扶贫是大政策，大政策还要细化，就像绣花一样。不同的地方、不同的贫困户有不同的扶法，新疆南疆是一种扶法，石漠化地区是一种扶法，太行山是一种扶法，青海三江源是一种扶法，大小凉山又是一种扶法，对民族地区、游牧地区、“直过民族”地区，对语言不通的地方和语言通的地方，对文化背景不同的地方，工作要因地制宜。可以多提供一些脱贫攻坚工作方面的好经验好做法，给大家启发。

Speaking of regional differences, Xi Jinping points out that today region-wide poverty alleviation – for instance the whole of northwest or northeast China – is no longer a problem. The focus should shift to segmented zones within the large regions. Poverty alleviation is a general policy, and detailed rules for implementation should be worked out, like doing elaborate embroidery.

Different measures should be applied to different localities and impoverished households. These include southern Xinjiang, stony deserts, the Taihang Mountains, the source region of the Yangtze, Yellow and Lancang rivers in southern Qinghai, the Greater and Lesser Liangshan Mountains, ethnic minority areas and grasslands, areas inhabited by the ethnic groups that have crossed stages of development to directly enter socialism, areas with different cultural backgrounds, and areas where standard Chinese language is not widely used. Good experience and methods of poverty elimination may be provided to inspire new ideas.

综合施策

2016年8月，习近平在青海调研考察时指出，脱贫攻坚要坚持精准扶贫、精准脱贫，切实做到脱真贫、真脱贫。要综合施策、打好组合拳，做到多政策、多途径、多方式综合发力。要通过改变生存环境、提高生活水平、提高生产能力实现脱贫，还要有巩固脱贫的后续计划、措施、保障。这些论述阐明了“精准扶贫”综合施策的特点与要义，即通过“综合手段”和“全程干预”实现脱贫攻坚的多重目标，同时通过严格的考核来保障相关政策的落实。

例如，在政策层面，《中共中央 国务院关于打赢脱贫攻坚战的决定》提出，实施健康扶贫工程，保障贫困人口享有基本医疗卫生服务，努力防止因病致贫、因病返贫。就是通过综合施策，形成政策合力，突出问题导向，实施精准扶贫，有效防止因病致贫返贫。

Holistic Approaches to Poverty Elimination

When talking to local people during his visit to Qinghai Province in August 2016, Xi Jinping reiterated the importance of targeted poverty elimination and earnest efforts to deliver assistance to those in need. He stressed the synergy of different policies and channels. Efforts should be made to improve local living environment, raise the local living standard, and enhance people's ability to work, and follow-up plans and measures are also needed to sustain the results of poverty elimination. These views highlight holistic approaches and whole-process control to realize multiple goals in poverty elimination, and strict review to ensure enforcement of relevant policies.

In accordance with the Decision on Winning the Battle Against Poverty, China will carry out poverty relief projects through better healthcare. Impoverished people will have access to basic medical services, and efforts will be made to prevent them from slipping back into poverty because of illness.

贫困县全部摘帽

1986年，中国政府组建专门的扶贫开发工作机构，开启了政府主导的开发式扶贫事业。国务院贫困地区经济开发领导小组按照严格标准在全国范围内识别出331个国家级贫困县，此后根据各时期扶贫开发形势的变化，先后三次调整了国家扶贫开发工作重点县名单。2011年，《中国农村扶贫开发规划纲要（2011—2020年）》颁布实施，国务院扶贫开发领导小组公布新一轮国定扶贫开发工作重点县和集中连片特困地区县，前者592个，后者680个，剔除重合部分，两者合计832个县，构成了脱贫攻坚战需要脱贫摘帽的县。

新时期脱贫攻坚目标是到2020年实现“两个确保”，即确保农村贫困人口实现脱贫、确保贫困县全部脱贫摘帽。2016年习近平在重庆调研时强调：“脱贫摘帽要坚持成熟一个摘一个，既防止不思进取、等靠要，又防止揠苗助长、图虚名。”2016年全国共有28个贫困县提出退出申请，其中

Lifting All Poor Counties Out of Poverty

China set up a special organization in 1986 to take charge of development-oriented poverty alleviation. This organization, the State Council Leading Group for Economic Development of Poor Regions, identified 331 poor counties across the country, and the list was subsequently adjusted three times based on changing conditions.

In 2011, the Outline for Development-oriented Poverty Alleviation of China's Rural Areas (2011-2020) was released, and the updated list of 592 key poor counties and 680 ones in contiguous areas of extreme poverty – the total number being 832 after removing overlaps. They are the focus of state assistance to eliminate poverty.

By 2020, all rural poor population and poor counties are to be lifted out of poverty.

During an inspection tour in Chongqing in 2016, Xi Jinping pointed out that poor counties would be removed from the poverty list one by one once they had escaped poverty. These counties must neither be content with the status quo and wait for outside assistance, nor seek unwarranted credit by "pulling up seedlings to help them grow."

In 2016, 28 poor counties applied to be removed from the poverty list. Among them

江西省井冈山市、河南省兰考县率先通过国家专项评估检查，分别于2017年2月25日、27日由省级政府批准退出。2017年首批申请退出的28个贫困县脱贫摘帽，既是1986年国家设定贫困县以来第一次实现贫困县数量净减少，也是实现贫困县全部摘帽目标的良好起步，为今后几年贫困县退出树立了标杆、作出了示范。截至2020年2月底，全国832个贫困县中已有601个宣布摘帽，179个正在进行退出检查，还有52个贫困县即将摘帽，区域性整体贫困基本得到解决。

Jinggangshan City of Jiangxi Province and Lankao County of Henan Province were the first to pass national evaluation reviews, and quit the list on February 25 and 27, 2017 respectively. With the 28 counties being removed from the poverty list, for the first time since 1986, China saw a net decrease in the number of poor counties. This set a good example for other poor counties to follow suit.

By late February 2020, 601 of China's 832 poor counties had announced to have eliminated poverty, 179 were going through national evaluation reviews, and the remaining 52 were expecting to be removed from the poverty list soon. Overall regional poverty has been basically eliminated throughout the country.

摘帽不摘政策

一些贫困县摘帽后，出现了松劲懈怠现象，有的撤摊子、歇歇脚，有的转移重心、更换频道，有的书记、县长希望动一动，一些已脱贫的群众收入不再增加甚至下降。对此，习近平要求，贫困县摘帽后，要继续完成剩余贫困人口脱贫任务，实现已脱贫人口的稳定脱贫；贫困县党政正职要保持稳定，做到摘帽不摘责任；脱贫攻坚主要政策要继续执行，做到摘帽不摘政策；扶贫工作队不能撤，做到摘帽不摘帮扶；要把防止返贫放在重要位置，做到摘帽不摘监管；有关部门要抓紧研究提出落实意见。

Poverty Relief Policies Continue After Counties Being Removed from Poverty List.

After being removed from the poverty list, some once-poor counties have slackened their efforts. Some have abandoned their policies and withdrawn their work teams, some want to take a break, and others tend to shift their focus or change ways of development. Some county Party committee secretaries and county mayors want to transfer to other work posts. Some once-poor people find their incomes have stagnated or are even decreasing.

Seeing these problems, Xi Jinping demands that after being removed from poverty list, the former poor counties must continue to help their remaining poor populations escape poverty and ensure they do not slip back into poverty. Their county Party committee secretaries and county mayors should remain steadfast in their posts, and not shirk their responsibilities, major poverty relief policies will continue, and work teams must not withdraw but continue their assistance. Every effort must be made to prevent people from falling back into poverty, and relevant supervision must continue. He also requires relevant government departments to work out measures for implementing the above instructions.

驻村帮扶

精准扶贫和脱贫攻坚的关键是人。中国的扶贫工作进入了精准扶贫时代，驻村帮扶在精准扶贫中发挥了无可替代的作用。2013年，在《关于创新机制扎实推进农村扶贫开发工作的意见》中，国家提出将健全干部驻村帮扶机制作为六项扶贫开发工作机制创新之一，要求在各省（自治区、直辖市）现有工作基础上，普遍建立驻村工作队（组）制度。确保每个贫困村都有驻村工作队（组），每个贫困户都有帮扶责任人。2014年3月，国务院扶贫开发领导小组召开第二次全体会议，进一步要求各地把驻村帮扶工作和第二批党的群众路线教育实践活动结合起来，认真总结现有帮扶经验，选拔有经验、有能力、懂扶贫、善于同农民打交道的干部，在2014年上半年派驻到每个贫困村。

其主要作用体现在：第一，驻村帮扶完善了贫困村的治理结构。在缺少监督的情况下，扶贫资源分配中优亲厚友的现象比较普遍，这影响了干群关系，也影响

Resident Work Teams in Poor Villages

People are the key factor in China's poverty alleviation and elimination. The resident work teams dispatched to help poor villages play an irreplaceable role in targeted alleviation.

According to the central leadership's Decision on Creating New Mechanisms for Promoting Rural Poverty Alleviation and Development in 2013, dispatching resident work teams was one of the six mechanisms to be adopted across the country. Every poor village would have one resident work team, and every poor household would have one person designated to help them.

At its second plenary meeting in March 2014, the State Council Leading Group of Poverty Alleviation and Development decided to combine the work of resident work teams with the CPC's campaign to educate Party members about keeping close ties with the villagers. Based on a summary of current experience, capable and experienced officials who understood poverty alleviation and were adept at communicating with farmers were dispatched to every poor village in the first half of 2014.

First, the work teams have helped improve village management. Due to a lack of supervision, there had been cases where

了扶贫的效果。驻村帮扶的工作队员来自村庄之外，他们与村庄没有直接的利益关联，这保证了驻村工作队可以在村庄中以客观公正的身份参与村庄事务。在贫困户识别、扶贫资源使用和产业发展中，驻村工作队和村级组织既相互配合，又相互监督，从而改善了村级治理格局。第二，驻村帮扶实现了更有效的扶贫资源动员。驻村帮扶工作队来自上级机关，具有更强的资源动员能力，他们的加入大大增加了贫困村的帮扶资源。第三，驻村帮扶推动了贫困村的产业发展和脱贫攻坚任务的完成。在进驻贫困村以后，驻村帮扶工作队都会根据贫困村的特点和问题，深入分析其致贫原因，并提出相应的发展规划，包括基础设施发展、产业发展和农民文化设施建设。在驻村帮扶工作队的支持下，贫困村形成了脱贫发展的策略和因户施策的扶贫方案。

poverty relief resources were distributed in favor of relatives and friends of village heads rather than to those really in need, which weakened the ties between village heads and villagers and affected the results of poverty alleviation. Since the work team members are all outsiders who have no direct interest connection with the villages, they can take an objective and just stance in village management. The work teams and the village management committees work together in identifying poor households, using relief resources, and developing economic activities, and they supervise each other in this process, thus improving village management.

Second, the work teams have helped with effective mobilization of relief resources. Since these teams come from higher levels of authority, they are better able to mobilize relief resources, and can bring more of such resources to the villages.

Third, the work teams have promoted new economic activities, and supported development and the completion of relief tasks in poor villages. They generally conduct an in-depth analysis of the features of the poor villages and the causes of their poverty, and then work out corresponding plans for infrastructure and cultural facilities and new economic activities. With the support of these teams, the poor villages have adopted relevant tactics and specific plans for individual households.

| 汉英对照 |

精准脱贫篇

Targeted Poverty Elimination

中国关键词

KEYWORDS TO UNDERSTAND CHINA

权 威 解 读 当 代 中 国

中国外文出版发行事业局（CIPG）
当代中国与世界研究院（ACCWS）
中国翻译研究院（CATL）

新世界出版社
NEW WORLD PRESS

Contents
目 录

坚持加大投入，强化资金支持
Increasing Inputs and Financial Support

基本公共服务
Basic Public Services 204

稳定脱贫长效机制
Long-Term Mechanism for Stable Poverty Elimination 210

“两线合一”
Unifying Two Standards 214

整合涉农资金
Integrating Government Funds for Rural Development 218

易地搬迁扶贫
Relocation of Rural Poor for Poverty Alleviation 222

社会保障兜底
Improving Social Security for Poverty Alleviation 224

医疗保险和医疗救助脱贫
Medical Insurance and Medical Aid for Poverty Elimination 228

健康扶贫
The Health Program for Poverty Alleviation 232

公益岗位扶贫
Welfare Jobs for Poverty Alleviation.. 236

专项扶贫
Special Poverty Alleviation Programs 238

金融扶贫
Financial Measures for Poverty Alleviation 242

城乡建设用地增减挂钩
Exchanging Newly Added Cropland Quotas with the Land for Construction 244

坚持社会动员，凝聚各方力量
Mobilizing Society and Pooling Strengths of All Sectors

消除贫困是社会主义本质要求
Eliminating Poverty: a Fundamental Task for Socialism.......................... 248

脱贫攻坚是以人民为中心发展思想的重要体现
Poverty Elimination: a People-Centered Approach to Development 252

获得感
A Sense of Gain 256

大扶贫格局
An All-Encompassing Campaign Against Poverty............................ 258

定点扶贫
Paired-Up Assistance in Poverty Alleviation 262

社会扶贫
Social Assistance in Poverty Alleviation 268

东西部扶贫协作
East-West Cooperation in Poverty Alleviation 270

坚持从严要求，促进真抓实干
Strict Standards for Practical Progress

底线任务
Bottom-Line Tasks for Achieving Moderate Prosperity....................... 278

"扶真贫、真扶贫"
Helping Those in Need and Delivering Genuine Outcomes........................280

提高脱贫质量
Enhancing the Effectiveness of Poverty Elimination 284

干部轮训
Rotation Training of Officials............286

脱贫攻坚责任书
Poverty Elimination Pledges 288

中央统筹、省负总责、市县抓落实
A Mechanism of Defined Responsibilities 292

"绣花"功夫
"Being Meticulous Like Doing Embroidery" 296

阳光扶贫
Transparency in Poverty Alleviation...300

第三方评估机制
Third Party Evaluation.....................304

扶贫领域腐败和作风问题专项治理
Rectification of Corruption and Misconduct in Poverty Alleviation.....308

最严格的考核评估
Strictest Review and Evaluation of Poverty Elimination........................310

坚持群众主体，激发内生动力

Motivating the People as the Main Actors

开发式扶贫

Development-Oriented Poverty Alleviation 318

内生动力

Internal Impetus for Poverty Elimination 322

扶贫同扶志扶智结合

Poverty Alleviation Through Increasing People's Confidence and Helping Them Acquire Knowledge and Skills 326

产业扶贫

Poverty Alleviation Through Creating New Economic Activity 330

光伏扶贫

Photovoltage Projects for Poverty Alleviation 334

教育扶贫

Poverty Alleviation Through Education 338

携手消除贫困，共建人类命运共同体

Joining Hands to End Poverty and Build a Global Community with a Shared Future

联合国千年发展目标

Millennium Development Goals........344

南南合作

South-South Cooperation...............346

没有贫困的人类命运共同体

A Poverty-Free Global Community with a Shared Future......................350

坚持加大投入，强化资金支持

Increasing Inputs and Financial Support

基本公共服务

基本公共服务是指建立在一定社会共识基础上，根据一国经济社会发展阶段和总体水平，为维持本国经济社会的稳定的、基本的社会正义和凝聚力，保护个人最基本的生存权和发展权，为实现人的全面发展所需要的基本社会条件。基本公共服务包括三个要点：一是保障人类的基本生存权（或生存的基本需要），为了实现这个目标，需要政府及社会为每个人都提供基本就业保障、基本养老保障、基本生活保障等；二是满足基本尊严（或体面）和基本能力的需要，需要政府及社会为每个人都提供基本的教育和文化服务；三是满足基本健康的需要，需要政府及社会为每个人都提供基本的健康保障。随着经济发展和人民生活水平的提高，一个社会基本公共服务的范围会逐步扩展，水平也会逐步提高。

中共十八大报告提出，到2020年基本公共服务均等化总体实现。2017年3月，

Basic Public Services

Basic public services reflect a social consensus and a country's economic and social development. They maintain stability, basic justice and cohesion, ensure people's rights to basic subsistence and development, and guarantee them opportunities for all-round development.

There are three essentials for basic public services. The first is to protect the right to subsistence (or survival needs) of human beings. To realize this, the government and society need to provide some form of employment, a pension, and basic living conditions. The second is to satisfy people's needs to maintain dignity and the ability to participate in society. For this purpose, the government and society need to provide basic education and cultural services for every citizen. The third is to meet basic health needs and provide health services for all.

The scope of public services will gradually expand along with economic development and general improvements to living standards.

In the report to the 18th National Congress, the CPC set the goal of generally achieving equal access to basic public services by 2020. The Plan on Promoting Equal Access to Basic Public Services During the 13th Five-year Plan Period, issued by the State Council in March 2017, defined their

国务院印发《“十三五”推进基本公共服务均等化规划》，界定了基本公共服务范围，包括保障基本民生需求的教育、就业、社会保障、医疗卫生、住房保障、文化体育等领域的公共服务。脱贫攻坚目标之一，是实现贫困地区基本公共服务均等化。2018年2月12日，习近平在打好精准脱贫攻坚战座谈会上指出，脱贫攻坚的目标是，确保到2020年现行标准下农村贫困人口全部脱贫，消除绝对贫困；确保贫困县全部摘帽，解决区域性整体贫困。稳定实现贫困人口“两不愁三保障”，贫困地区基本公共服务领域主要指标接近全国水平。2018年6月15日，中共中央、国务院出台的《关于打赢脱贫攻坚战三年行动的指导意见》明确提出，实现贫困地区基本公共服务主要领域指标接近全国平均水平，主要有：贫困地区具备条件的乡镇和建制村通硬化路，贫困村全部实现通动力电，全面解决贫困人口住房和饮水安全问题，贫困村达到人居环境干净整洁的基本要求，切实解决义务教育学生因贫失学辍学问题，基本养老保险和基本医疗保险、大病保险实现

scope as including education, employment, social security, medical and public health services, housing, cultural and sports services.

Addressing a seminar on targeted poverty elimination held on February 12, 2018, Xi Jinping defined the goals for the year 2020 as: to lift all rural population living under current poverty line out of poverty and eliminate absolute poverty; help all poor counties escape poverty and eliminate overall regional poverty; and guarantee food and clothing to those living in poverty, ensure they have proper access to compulsory education, basic medical services and safe housing, and ensure the main indicators of basic public services be close to the national average.

According to the Three-year Guideline on Winning the Battle Against Poverty, released by the central authorities on June 15, 2018, the main indicators of basic public services include:

- Towns, townships and villages in poor areas have asphalt roads where conditions permit;
- Poor villages all have three-phase power;
- Poor population have housing and safe drinking water;
- Poor villages have clean living environments;
- No child entitled to compulsory education should drop out of school;
- Poor population are all covered by

贫困人口全覆盖，最低生活保障实现应保尽保。集中连片特困地区和革命老区、民族地区、边疆地区发展环境明显改善，深度贫困地区如期完成全面脱贫任务。

the basic old-age insurance, basic medical insurance and serious illness insurance;

- All eligible people have subsistence allowances;
- Contiguous areas of extreme poverty, old revolutionary base areas, areas with large ethnic minority populations and border areas all see their development conditions notably improved; and
- Severely impoverished areas have escaped poverty as scheduled.

稳定脱贫长效机制

贫困具有长期和动态的特征。所谓稳定脱贫，是指通过创新观念、激活动力、稳定收入来源、完善基础设施、提升公共服务等方式，降低脱贫群体的脆弱性，增强其发展能力，不断改善其生活水平，永久跳出“贫困陷阱”。建立健全稳定脱贫长效机制不仅能够消除一家一户的绝对贫困，促进贫困地区经济社会的可持续发展，而且有助于阻断贫困的代际传递。建立健全稳定脱贫的长效机制，不仅影响打赢脱贫攻坚战的进程与质量，而且对于2020年后促进贫困地区经济社会可持续发展、减缓相对贫困，为实现第二个百年目标奠定基础，也具有重要意义。

对此，习近平指出，要把防止返贫摆在重要位置，适时组织对脱贫人口开展“回头看”，对返贫人口和新发生贫困人口及

Long-Term Mechanism for Stable Poverty Elimination

Poverty is a state that may last indefinitely. Stable poverty elimination means that the people who have escaped poverty now have more initiative, stable sources of income, and better infrastructure and public services. They are less vulnerable, as they have more ability to manage their own development and improve living standards, and can escape the "poverty pitfall" permanently.

A sound long-term mechanism for stable poverty elimination will help individual households eliminate absolute poverty, promote sustainable economic and social development of poor areas, and stop intergenerational transmission of poverty. While influencing the progress and quality of poverty elimination, it will also be significant to poor areas in maintaining sustainable economic and social development and in mitigating relative poverty after 2020, thus laying a solid foundation for realizing China's second centenary goal by the mid-21st century.

Xi Jinping has demanded action to prevent people from falling back into poverty. He has required follow-up checks at appropriate intervals and timely assistance to any new victims of poverty and those

时予以帮扶。要探索建立稳定脱贫长效机制，强化产业扶贫，组织消费扶贫，加大培训力度，促进转移就业，让贫困群众有稳定的工作岗位。要做好易地扶贫搬迁后续帮扶，加强扶贫同扶志扶智相结合，让脱贫具有可持续的内生动力。

who fall back into poverty. With a long-term mechanism for stable poverty elimination in place, the poor can benefit from economic development, earn more from selling their products and services, receive more training, and find stable jobs other than farming. Assistance will continue after relocation, and the poor will have more confidence in their ability to escape poverty and acquire the skills they need to do so, so that poverty elimination will be sustained through the endogenous initiative of the poor themselves.

"两线合一"

2007年1月，中央一号文件要求"在全国范围建立农村最低生活保障制度"，中国自此形成了以低保和扶贫开发两大制度为主干的农村扶贫新格局。低保与扶贫开发都是农村扶贫减贫和脱贫工作的基本制度安排，两项制度各具特点和制度优势，可以形成政策效应互补的帮扶合力，在整体上提升农村反贫困效果。

然而，低保和扶贫开发是两项不同的制度安排，两项制度形成的历史路径不一，且有着不同的政策目标和政策手段。因此，切实做好低保和扶贫开发两项制度的分工协调和有效衔接，成为打赢脱贫攻坚战的重要决策部署。《关于做好农村最低生活保障制度与扶贫开发政策有效衔接的指导意见》要求，农村低保标准低于国家扶贫标准的地方，要按照国家扶贫标准综合确定农村低保的最低指导标准，农村低保标准已经达到国家扶贫标准的地方，要根据动态调整机制科学调整。

所谓"两线合一"，就是实现低保标准和扶贫标准的统一。自2016年1月起，农村低保标准达到每人每年2808元，与扶贫标准相一致，实现了"两线合一"，并根据

Unifying Two Standards

The No.1 Document issued by the central leadership in January 2007 required the establishment of a rural subsistence allowance system nationwide. This launched a new rural poverty alleviation structure supported by both the subsistence allowance system and development-oriented poverty alleviation.

These two systems have different features and strengths, and their integration will build synergy in providing assistance to those in need, and enhance the impact of anti-poverty efforts in rural areas. As they were originally formed in different historic conditions with different policy goals and means, good planning is needed to coordinate the two systems for effective results.

According to a document released by the central authorities on linking these two systems, where the rural subsistence allowance is lower than the national poverty alleviation allowance, the former will be raised to the level of the latter; where the former has reached the level of the latter, rational adjustments may be made if necessary. In this way, the two standards will be roughly unified.

Since 2016, the level of rural subsistence allowance has been raised to 2,808 yuan per person per year, the same as the national poverty alleviation allowance, and the figure

物价上涨水平每年进行调整。农村低保标准与扶贫标准同步提高，保障贫困家庭基本生活水平与全面建成小康社会相适应，主要是通过以下三条途径来实现的：一是对有一定收入的低保家庭，据实核算家庭成员年人均收入，按照人数足额补差；二是对无劳动能力、无任何收入的低保对象，按照当地低保标准全额补助；三是对充分享受低保政策，足额领取低保补助金后，生活仍有较大困难的家庭，通过临时救助帮助解决生活困难。

will be adjusted in accordance with price rises every year. The living standards of poor households thus will grow in parallel with the country's overall progress in building a moderately prosperous society.

There are three ways to synchronize these measures.

(1) For households living on subsistence allowances despite other income, the per-capita yearly income of their family members will be calculated and any of the deficit will be made up;

(2) For people living on subsistence allowances who have no ability to work and no income at all, full allowances will be provided in line with local subsistence allowance standards; and

(3) For those who still experience severe difficulties even after receiving the subsistence allowances, temporary assistance will be provided to mitigate their problems.

整合涉农资金

在各级财政扶贫投入规模不断增加的情况下，贫困地区统筹安排使用扶贫资金却面临着一些难题。比如，由于上下权责不匹配，贫困县没有项目安排和资金使用自主权，“基层最知道自己哪儿疼，却没法开方抓药”；又如，由于专款专用的规定，“打酱油的钱不能买醋”，一定程度上造成项目和资金“碎片化”使用，制约了精准扶贫措施的成效。

针对这些问题，《中共中央 国务院关于打赢脱贫攻坚战的决定》明确提出，“建立健全脱贫攻坚多规划衔接、多部门协调长效机制，整合目标相近、方向类同的涉农资金。按照权责一致原则，支持连片特困地区县和国家扶贫开发工作重点县围绕本县突出问题，以扶贫规划为引领，以重点扶贫项目为平台，把专项扶贫资金、相关涉农资金和社会帮扶资金捆绑集中使用”。支持贫困县统筹整合使用财政涉农资金，既是提高财政资金配置效率、保障脱贫攻坚资金需求的关键之举，也是深化农

Integrating Government Funds for Rural Development

As they receive more poverty relief funds from the governments, poor areas often find problems in using the money. One problem is a lack of autonomy in arranging projects and using funds. Poor counties know where the money is needed the most, but do not necessarily have the power to use the money for that purpose. Under the rule that a fund can be used for its specified purpose only and cannot be diverted for other purposes, to some extent, projects and funds are "fragmented," and this impacts the results of targeted poverty alleviation measures.

To address these problems, the Decision on Winning the Battle Against Poverty proposed a long-term mechanism for docking different plans for poverty elimination, coordinating government departments, and integrating funds with similar purposes in agricultural development. In line with the principle of balance between power and responsibility, counties in contiguous areas of extreme poverty and key counties eligible for state assistance will focus on their own most prominent problems, follow poverty alleviation plans, and coordinate the application of special funds allocated for poverty relief, funds for agricultural development, and social

村改革、加快实现农业现代化的重大探索。

2016年，国务院办公厅印发《关于支持贫困县开展统筹整合使用财政涉农资金试点的意见》，旨在通过试点，形成“多个渠道引水、一个龙头放水”的扶贫投入新格局，激发贫困县内生动力，支持贫困县围绕突出问题，以摘帽销号为目标，以脱贫成效为导向，以扶贫规划为引领，以重点扶贫项目为平台，统筹整合使用财政涉农资金，撬动金融资本和社会帮扶资金投入扶贫开发，提高资金使用精准度和效益，确保如期完成脱贫攻坚任务。

assistance funds on key projects. This will enhance the efficiency of fund utilization to meet urgent capital needs. It will also drive rural reform to a deeper level and accelerate agricultural modernization.

The State Council issued in 2016 a document allowing some pilot priority counties to combine government funds for rural development. These trials are expected to create a new scheme of poverty relief inputs, by "diverting water from multiple sources and drawing it off through a single tap," so as to increase the internal impetus of poor counties, enhance the efficiency of various funds in developing key projects, and divert more capital and social assistance resources into poverty elimination.

易地搬迁扶贫

易地搬迁是“五个一批”精准脱贫的重要内容，是中共中央发出脱贫攻坚战总动员后的第一仗，也是中国打赢脱贫攻坚战的重要内容。《中共中央 国务院关于打赢脱贫攻坚战的决定》提出，实施易地搬迁脱贫，对居住在生存条件恶劣、生态环境脆弱、自然灾害频发等地区的农村贫困人口，加快实施易地扶贫搬迁工程。

易地搬迁属于生态扶贫和绿色减贫的范畴，其主要原因就是易地搬迁应遵循自然规律与经济规律，对于生态环境较差的地区，实施保护型减贫策略，通过搬迁、因地制宜确定安置方式来改善贫困人口的客观生存环境，有效缓解扶贫开发造成的环境破坏，促进当地经济社会的可持续发展。根据规划，“十三五”时期中国将对约1000万建档立卡贫困人口实施易地扶贫搬迁。截至2019年年末，易地扶贫搬迁建设任务基本完成。

Relocation of Rural Poor for Poverty Alleviation

Relocating those living under adverse natural conditions is one of China's five targeted measures in battling poverty. The Decision on Winning the Battle Against Poverty provides special plans on accelerating the relocation of rural poor who live under unfavorable natural conditions, in fragile eco-environments, or in areas suffering frequent disasters.

This relocation is a green pathway as it follows the natural rules and dynamics of the economy. For areas with fragile eco-environments, conservation is a wise tactic to avoid further damage caused by development while improving the living conditions of the poor by removing them to better locations. This can effectively promote local sustainable economic and social development.

China planned to relocate 10 million people registered as living below the poverty line during the 13th Five-year Plan period (2016-2020). By the end of 2019, it had roughly completed this task.

社会保障兜底

社会保障兜底是“五个一批”工程的内容之一，指对贫困人口中完全或部分丧失劳动能力的人，由社会保障来兜底，统筹协调农村扶贫标准和农村低保标准，加大其他形式的社会救助力度，加强医疗保险和医疗救助，将新型农村合作医疗和大病保险政策向贫困人口倾斜。

《中共中央 国务院关于打赢脱贫攻坚战的决定》明确了“两不愁三保障”的脱贫攻坚目标。“三保障”的目标不仅是扶贫的新定位，也正视并提升了社会保障制度的地位，强化了完善社会保障制度建设的必要性。《决定》要求充分发挥社会保障减贫作用，提出一系列的社会保障减贫举措，特别强调开发式扶贫和农村低保制度

Improving Social Security for Poverty Alleviation

Improving social security is one of China's five targeted measures employed for poverty alleviation. The government will provide social security for poor people who have completely or partially lost the ability to work, unify the standards of rural poverty alleviation allowance and rural subsistence allowance, and increase other forms of social aid. It will also increase medical insurance and medical aid, and the new rural cooperative medical insurance and the serious illness insurance schemes will extend their scope to benefit the impoverished.

The Decision on Winning the Battle Against Poverty defined China's goals in poverty elimination as assuring the basic needs of food and clothing for those living in poverty and guaranteeing that they have access to compulsory education, basic medical services and safe housing. This elevates the importance of social security. The document also rolled out a range of measures for reducing poverty through social security, emphasized development-oriented poverty alleviation and the rural subsistence allowance system as China's strategic measures in the campaign against poverty, and required integration of these two

均是中国反贫困的重要战略举措，要求做好两项制度的衔接，2020年前确保贫困地区的低保标准逐步达到脱贫标准。

systems to ensure that all poor areas will see the standard of their subsistence allowance match that of national poverty alleviation allowance by the year 2020.

医疗保险和医疗救助脱贫

习近平在2016年全国卫生与健康大会上发表重要讲话时强调，“没有全民健康，就没有全面小康。要把人民健康放在优先发展的战略地位”。保障贫困人口的健康权利，让贫困人口看得起病，不至于因病致贫和因病返贫，对于脱贫攻坚至关重要。《中共中央 国务院关于打赢脱贫攻坚战的决定》明确提出，实施健康扶贫工程，保障贫困人口享有基本医疗卫生服务，努力防止因病致贫、因病返贫。

《关于实施健康扶贫工程的指导意见》提出，坚持精准扶贫、精准脱贫基本方略，与深化医药卫生体制改革紧密结合，针对农村贫困人口因病致贫、因病返贫问题，突出重点地区、重点人群、重点病种，进一步加强统筹协调和资源整合，采取有效措施提升农村贫困人口医疗保障水平和贫困地区医疗卫生服务能力，全面提高农村贫困人口健康水平，为农村贫困人口与全国人民一道迈入全面小康社会提供健康保障。为此，需要建立健全医疗保险

Medical Insurance and Medical Aid for Poverty Elimination

Speaking to the 2016 National Health Conference, Xi Jinping said, "We cannot achieve moderate prosperity in all respects if we cannot ensure the people's health. We must take health as a strategic priority in our development."

It is of vital importance to China's poverty elimination to ensure the health of the poor, and ensure that they can afford medical services and do not become poor or slip back to poverty again because of illness.

The Decision on Winning the Battle Against Poverty unveiled a health program to this end.

Another document, Guidelines on Implementing the Health Program for Poverty Alleviation, instructed that targeted poverty alleviation and elimination should be integrated with further healthcare reform. Targeting the problems of rural people who become poor or return to poverty because of illnesses, and targeting the key areas, key groups and key illnesses, efforts will be made to coordinate work and integrate resources, and effective measures will be taken to improve medical services to the rural poor and in poor areas, leading to an overall improvement in the health of the poor.

和医疗救助制度，加大医疗救助、临时救助、慈善救助等帮扶力度，保障贫困人口享有基本医疗卫生服务。

Relevant systems for medical insurance and medical aid will be improved, with more medical, temporary and charity aid, and the poor will have access to basic medical and health services.

健康扶贫

国务院扶贫办建档立卡数据显示，截至2015年年底，因病致贫、因病返贫的贫困人口近2000万人，占贫困人口总数的44.1%。其中，患大病的和慢性病的是734万人。在各种致贫原因中，因病致贫在各地区都排在最前面。健康不良的状态容易导致贫困，贫困又容易滋生疾病，贫困人口极易陷入“疾病—贫困—疾病”的恶性循环。

因此，保障贫困人口的健康权利，防止因病致贫、因病返贫，开展健康扶贫，成为脱贫攻坚的重点领域。健康扶贫是国家精准扶贫精准脱贫方略的重要组成部分，是确保打赢脱贫攻坚战、实现全面建成小康社会目标的重要举措。为此，国家卫生计生委、国务院扶贫办等部门联合印发《关于实施健康扶贫工程的指导意见》，强调健康扶贫工程要按照脱贫攻坚战“两不愁三保障”的要求，聚焦贫困人口“基本医疗有保障”这一总体目标，落实健康

The Health Program for Poverty Alleviation

According to the State Council Leading Group Office of Poverty Alleviation and Development, nearly 20 million people in China were victims of poverty or had returned to poverty because of illness by the end of 2015, accounting for 44.1 percent of the total number of poor population. Illness was the main cause of poverty. Of this total, 7.34 million had serious or chronic illnesses. Bad health may cause poverty, and poverty can in turn lead to bad health, thus forming a vicious cycle of "illness – poverty – illness" among the poor.

Naturally, protecting these people's right to health, preventing them from being trapped in or returning to poverty because of illness, and launching a health program are therefore very important features of China's poverty alleviation effort. The health program is part of China's targeted poverty elimination strategy, and an important measure to win the battle against poverty and achieve moderate prosperity in all respects.

In response to this, relevant government departments worked out the Guidelines on Implementing the Health Program for Poverty Alleviation. The program echoes China's poverty alleviation goal of guaranteeing access to basic medical services, the Healthy

中国和乡村振兴两大战略，通过大病集中救治一批、慢病签约服务管理一批、重病兜底保障一批“三个一批”行动计划，努力让贫困人口“看得起病、看得好病、看得上病、少生病”。

China initiative and the strategy of rural revitalization. Efforts will be made to ensure that the poor can afford medical services and seldom fall ill, as they can expect help from serious illness insurance and chronic illness services, and government funds will cover the remaining cost of critical ailments after the relevant reimbursements.

公益岗位扶贫

公益性岗位扶贫，是指在贫困地区特别是贫困村庄，设置一批公益性岗位，运用政府购买服务的理念和方式，给予现金或实物补贴，实现贫困人口的就业和增收，同时增加村庄和当地的公共服务供给。公益岗位扶贫的独特性表现在以下几个方面：

一是强制性。贫困劳动力必须保质保量完成规定任务才能获得相应收入，这避免了不劳而获，有效解决了贫困治理中的福利依赖和负向刺激问题。

二是兼职性。贫困劳动力按照岗位要求可以不定期地、自主灵活地完成工作量，这与他们的闲暇时间相适应。

三是非技术性。公益性岗位对劳动力的要求相对宽松，这与贫困劳动力的受教育水平相适应。

四是公益性。公益性岗位的职责必须是保障公共利益的服务内容，这与乡村治理的公共性诉求不谋而合。

Welfare Jobs for Poverty Alleviation

Jobs that are welfare in nature are created especially for the impoverished people in poor villages and poor regions, so that they can support themselves while improving local public services as the government will buy their services with cash or benefits in kind.

Welfare jobs have the following features:

(1) Compulsory: The workers must fulfill their tasks in both quality and quantity before receiving payment. This solves the problem of "reaping without sowing" and avoids welfare dependency and negative stimulus in managing poverty;

(2) Part-time: The workers can manage their work for certain posts flexibly during their spare time;

(3) Non-technical: The welfare jobs generally require few technical skills and match the workers' educational level; and

(4) Welfare nature: The jobs are part of public services and help improve village management.

专项扶贫

专项扶贫是指专门针对贫困人口和贫困问题而设计实施的开发式扶贫政策措施。20世纪80年代初期，国家开始启动实施“三西”农业建设计划和以工代赈计划。此后，专项扶贫是指依托发展资金、以工代赈资金、少数民族发展资金、“三西”农业建设专项补助资金、扶贫贷款贴息资金等财政专项扶贫资金而组织实施的扶贫工作。

与行业扶贫、社会扶贫所不同的是，专项扶贫的主要特点在于:（1）专项扶贫所需资金，主要来源于中央和地方预算安排的财政扶贫资金;（2）专项扶贫的实施一般采用项目形式（或单一项目，或综合性项目）;（3）专项扶贫项目实施，原则上要求到村到户，使真正的贫困村、贫困户直接受益;（4）组织实施专项扶贫的行

Special Poverty Alleviation Programs

Special poverty alleviation programs are development-oriented, especially designed and implemented to help the poor tackle poverty problems.

In the early 1980s, the state launched an agricultural development program and a work-relief plan for the poor counties in Gansu Province and Ningxia Hui Autonomous Region. Later, special programs were related to poverty alleviation work supported by development funds, work-relief funds, development funds for minority ethnic groups, agricultural development subsidies, and government-subsided discount loans for poverty alleviation projects.

As distinct from poverty alleviation through business development or with social assistance, special programs have the following features:

(1) The money needed mainly comes from the poverty relief funds appropriated from central and local budgets;

(2) Single or comprehensive projects are usually conducted to boost alleviation;

(3) The projects must be undertaken in the villages and by the households to ensure the truly impoverished are the direct beneficiaries; and

(4) The organizations in charge of project

政机构是各级政府扶贫开发领导小组及其办公室，同时还包括各级发展和改革委员会、财政部门等。

2011年，中共中央、国务院颁布实施《中国农村扶贫开发纲要（2011—2020年）》，正式将扶贫开发工作划分为专项扶贫、行业扶贫、社会扶贫三大块，其中专项扶贫主要包括易地扶贫搬迁、整村推进、以工代赈、产业扶贫、就业促进等内容。2015年，《中共中央 国务院关于打赢脱贫攻坚战的决定》进一步提出，强化政府责任，引领市场、社会协同发力，鼓励先富帮后富，构建专项扶贫、行业扶贫、社会扶贫互为补充的大扶贫格局。

implementation include poverty alleviation leading groups and their offices, development and reform commissions, and financial departments under all levels of government.

The Outline for Development-oriented Poverty Alleviation of China's Rural Areas (2011-2020), released in 2011, defines development-oriented poverty alleviation as special programs, corporate support, and social assistance. Special programs include relocation, village-based poverty alleviation, work-relief, business development, and employment improvement.

The Decision on Winning the Battle Against Poverty, issued in 2015, emphasizes the responsibilities of the government and the roles of the market and social assistance, and encourages those who have become better-off to help those still lagging behind, so as to build synergy by integrating special programs, corporate support and social assistance.

金融扶贫

金融扶贫是脱贫攻坚适应市场经济要求、拓展资金渠道的新举措，是扶贫投入的重大创新，是脱贫攻坚最强有力的支撑。具体来说，金融扶贫是指在中央政府主导下，各级政府、金融机构、各类企业或非企业社会组织参与扶贫开发，主要面向贫困地区和贫困人群提供综合金融服务，扶持低收入和贫困农户生产和经营，帮助其摆脱贫困、增加收入，实现自力更生，提高经济社会地位。

在长期扶贫开发探索和实践中，金融扶贫政策和机制不断完善和创新，从最开始实施扶贫贴息贷款到推广小额信贷（微型金融），从探索金融扶贫模式到初步形成金融扶贫政策体系，再到普惠金融、金融科技的发展支持下的精准扶贫战略，金融扶贫被越来越广泛地应用于中国扶贫开发的各个领域，在中国扶贫开发过程中发挥着越来越重要的作用。金融扶贫已成为推进中国扶贫开发的一项有效工具和重要手段。

Financial Measures for Poverty Alleviation

Financial measures are adopted in response to market demand. With more fund-raising channels, they help increase input and offer powerful support to China's poverty elimination campaign.

Under the guidance of the central authorities, local governments, financial institutions, enterprises and social organizations have played their roles in providing comprehensive financial services to poor areas and poor people, supporting low-income and poor rural households in production and business, and helping them escape poverty, increase income and enhance their economic and social status.

Relevant financial policies and mechanisms have improved, from soft loans to micro loans, from exploring the mode of financial assistance to devising a range of financial policies for poverty alleviation, and to targeted poverty alleviation supported by inclusive finance and financial technologies. Financial measures are applied extensively in China's development-oriented poverty relief, and have become an effective tool in the campaign of poverty alleviation.

城乡建设用地增减挂钩

城乡建设用地增减挂钩是土地利用的一大政策工具。这项政策在促进节约集约用地和城乡统筹发展中发挥了重要作用。所谓城乡建设用地增减挂钩，是指依据土地利用总体规划，将若干拟整理复垦为耕地的农村建设用地地块(即拆旧地块)和拟用于城镇建设的地块(即新建地块)等面积共同组成建新拆旧项目区(以下简称项目区)，通过建新拆旧和土地整理复垦等措施，在保证项目区内各类土地面积平衡的基础上，最终实现增加耕地有效面积，提高耕地质量，节约集约利用建设用地，更合理布局城乡用地的目标。

近年来，为支持扶贫开发，增减挂钩政策先后两次拓展范围，允许集中连片特困地区、国家级贫困县，以及省级贫困县的节余指标在省域内流转使用，这为贫困地区脱贫攻坚拓展了资金来源，有力推动了农村人居环境整治，促进了城乡公共服务均等化和区域均衡发展。

Exchanging Newly Added Cropland Quotas with the Land for Construction

China has created a policy tool that links newly added cropland quotas with the amount of land used for urban and rural construction. This helps support efficient use of land and integrated urban-rural development.

According to the overall plan on land use, the total area of the plots of land previously used for rural construction and now re-designated for farming and that of the land to be used for urban construction will be kept in balance, so as to ensure additional arable land with improved soil, efficient usage of construction land, and a rational configuration of urban and rural land.

In recent years, this policy has twice expanded in scope, and now allows the surplus quotas produced by the contiguous areas of extreme poverty, priority counties in national poverty alleviation, and provincial poor counties to be adjusted across provinces. The profits will be used to fight poverty and improve the rural living environment, equalize urban-rural access to public services, and balance regional development.

坚持社会动员，凝聚各方力量

Mobilizing Society and Pooling Strengths of All Sectors

消除贫困是社会主义本质要求

在2014年10月国务院召开的全国社会扶贫工作电视电话会议上，习近平指出，消除贫困，改善民生，逐步实现全体人民共同富裕，是社会主义的本质要求。2017年10月18日，习近平在中共十九大报告中指出，必须坚定不移把发展作为党执政兴国的第一要务，坚持解放和发展社会生产力，坚持社会主义市场经济改革方向，推动经济持续健康发展。

以邓小平同志为核心的中国共产党第二代中央领导集体探索并初步回答了“什么是社会主义、怎样建设社会主义”的问题。1992年初，邓小平在南方谈话中提出，“社会主义的本质，是解放生产力，发展生产力，消灭剥削，消除两极分化，最终达到共同富裕”。

社会主义本质论对实践具有重大的指导意义：（1）继承了科学社会主义的基本原则，是探索建设中国特色社会主义道路的最重大理论成果之一，是对马克思主义

Eliminating Poverty: a Fundamental Task for Socialism

Speaking to a national teleconference on poverty alleviation in October 2014, Xi Jinping said that eliminating poverty, improving living standards, and achieving common prosperity among all Chinese people is a fundamental task for socialism. In his report to the 19th CPC National Congress, he vowed to continue to pursue development as the Party's top priority in governance, unleash and develop the country's productive forces, continue reform to develop the socialist market economy, and promote sustained and sound economic growth.

The CPC's second generation of collective leadership with Deng Xiaoping at its core asked itself what socialism is and how to build socialism. During his tour to southern China in early 1992, Deng said, "The essence of socialism is liberation and development of the productive forces, elimination of exploitation and polarization, and the ultimate achievement of prosperity for all."

This vision guides China in four ways:

(1) It inherits the basic tenets of scientific socialism, and represents important theoretical progress in building Chinese socialism and a major development of Marxism;

的重大发展。（2）为我们既坚持公有制又完善和发展公有制指明了方向。（3）突破了把计划经济等一些原本不属于社会主义固有的东西当作社会主义本质特征的传统观念。（4）反映了人民的利益和时代的要求，澄清了不合乎时代进步和社会发展规律的模糊观念，摆脱了长期以来拘泥于具体模式而忽视社会主义本质的错误倾向，深化了对社会主义本质的认识。其内在要求是各级党政领导干部和广大人民群众树立科学的公平观和正义观，根本要求是解放和发展生产力。

(2) It charts the course for China in upholding and developing public ownership;

(3) It shatters the previous belief that mistakenly considered the planned economy as an inherent component of socialism; and

(4) It represents the people's interests and the requirement of the times, clarifies ambiguous thoughts that do not conform to the advance of the times and social development, abandons the long-existing erroneous tendency toward overemphasizing the stereotyped models and neglecting the nature of socialism, and improves people's perception of the nature of socialism.

It thereby guides Party and government officials and the general public with a correct view of equity and justice, and encourages the release and development of productive forces.

脱贫攻坚是以人民为中心发展思想的重要体现

在中共十八届五中全会上，习近平首次提出以人民为中心的发展思想。以人民为中心的发展思想，体现了中国共产党全心全意为人民服务的根本宗旨，体现了人民是推动发展的根本力量的唯物史观，体现了逐步实现共同富裕的目标要求。以人民为中心的发展思想，不能只停留在口头上、止步于思想环节，而要体现在经济社会发展各个环节。

在做好扶贫开发工作中，充分体现以人民为中心的发展思想，支持困难群众摆脱贫困，使发展成果更多更公平惠及全体人民，是中国共产党坚持全心全意为人民服务根本宗旨的重要体现，也是党和政府的职责所在。

习近平强调，脱贫攻坚必须依靠人民群众，组织和支持贫困群众自力更生，发挥人民群众主动性。要防止忽视贫困群众主体作用，贫困群众既是脱贫攻坚的对象，更是脱贫致富的主体。要注重扶贫同

Poverty Elimination: a People-Centered Approach to Development

Xi Jinping raised the idea of a people-centered approach to development at the fifth plenary session of the 18th CPC Central Committee. This approach echoes the CPC's founding mission of serving the people wholeheartedly, and reflects the belief that the people are the driving force behind development and the goal of common prosperity.

This must not fall victim to lip service or idle reflection, but be put into practice in all areas of social and economic development. In particular, it must be applied in helping the poor emerge from poverty, so that all the Chinese people can enjoy fully and fairly the benefits brought by development. This is where the duty of the CPC and the government lies.

Xi Jinping has emphasized the people's initiative in China's poverty elimination. Impoverished people are both the recipients of assistance and the main actors in fighting poverty. They must be motivated with more confidence, resolution and necessary skills to change their conditions, so that they will abandon the mindset of "others want me

扶志扶智相结合，把贫困群众的积极性和主动性充分调动起来，引导贫困群众树立主体意识，发扬自力更生精神，激发改变贫困面貌的干劲和决心，变“要我脱贫”为“我要脱贫”，靠自己的努力改变命运。

to fight poverty" and turn to "I want to fight poverty" and try to improve their lot through their own efforts.

获得感

获得感是指人们在收获某种物质或精神利益后而产生的满足感。2015年2月27日，习近平在中央全面深化改革领导小组第十次会议上首提这一概念。他指出，处理好改革“最先一公里”和“最后一公里”的关系，突破“中梗阻”，防止不作为，把改革方案的含金量充分展示出来，让人民群众有更多获得感。

获得感强调的是一种实实在在的客观“得到”，是“看得见、摸得着的实惠”，既包括物质方面，也包括精神方面。获得感的提出，使人民得到的利益有了进行指标衡量的可能，得到了人民群众的积极响应。“让人民群众有更多获得感”的提出，体现了中共十八大以来以习近平同志为核心的党中央立党为公、执政为民的宗旨意识，体现了坚持以人民为中心的发展思想，体现了社会建设要坚持共建共享的基本原则，体现了改革创新要以增进民生福祉为目标的价值导向。

A Sense of Gain

A "sense of gain" is the sense of satisfaction that people derive from obtaining some material or non-material gain. Xi Jinping raised this idea at the 10th meeting of the Leading Group for Further Reform Under the CPC Central Committee held on February 27, 2015. He demanded that the relationship between "the first mile" and "the last mile" of reform – the initiation and the implementation – be handled properly, removing obstacles, preventing nonfeasance, and demonstrating the highlights of reform plans, so as to give the people a stronger sense of gain.

A "sense of gain" emphasizes actual objective "gains," both material and non-material. This term made possible the use of measurable indicators of the gains obtained by the people, and received positive public response.

The suggestion to "enable the people to have a stronger sense of gain" demonstrates the CPC's commitment to its mission to serve the public and govern for the people, and its adherence to the people-centered approach to development. It demonstrates the fundamental principle that society must be built by all and to be enjoyed by all, and the guiding value that the aim of reform and innovation is to improve the wellbeing of the people.

大扶贫格局

“人心齐，泰山移”。脱贫致富不仅仅是贫困地区的事，也是全党全社会的共同责任，需要广泛动员和凝聚全社会力量，加快形成专项扶贫、行业扶贫、社会扶贫等多方力量、多种举措有机结合和互为支撑的“三位一体”大扶贫格局。

首先是强化东西部扶贫协作，引导东部地区加大对西部地区的帮扶力度。东部地区不仅要帮钱帮物，更要推动产业层面的合作，推动东部地区人才、资金、技术向贫困地区流动，充分发掘贫困地区的劳动力资源与自然资源优势，实现双方共赢；不仅要推动省级层面协作，而且要推动市县层面协作。其次是推进党政机关定点扶贫机制建设，支持各部门积极完成所承担的定点扶贫任务。近年来，中央和国家机关各部门、人民团体等承担定点扶贫任务的单位，围绕扶贫做了不少事情，为扶贫开发作出了重要贡献。今后的工作重点是围绕制度建设，明确各单位责任，建立考核评价机制。第三是鼓励国有企业承担更多扶贫开发任务。承担定点扶贫任务，是

An All-Encompassing Campaign Against Poverty

"United, we can move Mount Tai." This is an old Chinese saying about unity. To get rid of poverty is not the goal of poor areas alone. It is the shared mission of the CPC and Chinese society as a whole. Consequently, the whole of society needs to be mobilized, and special programs, corporate support and social assistance must be integrated to form synergy.

First, the east and the west strengthen cooperation, with the former increasing support to the latter. In addition to providing funds and material assistance, the east will work to promote economic development, increase the flow of human resources, capital and technologies to the west, and tap the workforce and natural resources of poor areas. Such cooperation can be conducted at the level of provinces, cities and counties.

Second, the Party and government departments and the people's organizations all have designated poverty alleviation tasks, with evaluation of their performance and results.

Third, state-owned enterprises are encouraged to take on more poverty alleviation

中央企业的政治责任，不能有丝毫含糊。

守望相助、扶危济困是中华民族的传统美德。今后，中国将继续深入研究、借鉴其他国家的成功做法，创新慈善事业制度，动员全社会力量广泛参与扶贫事业，鼓励支持各类企业、社会组织、个人参与到脱贫攻坚工作中来。同时，积极推动社会扶贫重心下沉，促进帮扶资源向贫困村和贫困户流动，实现同精准扶贫政策的有效对接。

work. This is a political duty that they must not shirk.

Helping each other, particularly helping those in need, is a great Chinese tradition. China will study and learn from other countries' successes, improve its charity system, and motivate enterprises, social organizations and individuals to participate extensively in poverty elimination. It will drive social involvement to the lower levels and communities and ensure that resources reach poor villages and poor households to achieve effective results.

定点扶贫

定点扶贫，是指党政机关、企事业单位和社会团体利用自己的资源，以贫困区域的重点贫困县为主要帮扶对象，与贫困地区合作以帮助其脱贫致富的一种开发式扶贫模式，其目的是促进党政机关、企事业单位和社会团体参与扶贫工作。这是中国特色扶贫开发工作的重要组成部分。2012年11月8日，国务院扶贫办、中组部等八部门联合印发《关于做好新一轮中央、国家机关和有关单位定点扶贫工作的通知》，确定了新一轮定点扶贫结对关系。参与定点扶贫的中央和国家机关等单位达到310个，第一次实现了定点扶贫工作对592个国家扶贫开发工作重点县的全覆盖。

依据定点扶贫工作介入点的不同，可以将实践中的不同扶贫方式分为：以项目扶持为介入点的扶贫模式、以产业开发为着力点的扶贫模式、以企业发展为推手的扶贫模式、以结对帮扶为手段的扶贫模式。

其一，以项目扶持为介入点的定点扶贫模式。在该模式下，定点扶贫主体以扶持适合当地发展项目的形式帮助其解决贫困问题。水利部在其定点贫困县开展以项

Paired-Up Assistance in Poverty Alleviation

Paired-up assistance is a unique practice in China's poverty alleviation. The CPC and government departments, enterprises, public institutions and social organizations are paired up with recipient poor counties to provide assistance to the latter. By using their own resources, these units can play their part in the national battle against poverty. This is an important element of China's poverty elimination campaign.

On November 8, 2012, the State Council Leading Group Office of Poverty Alleviation and Development and seven other government departments jointly released a notice on a new round of paired-up assistance by central departments and ministries, and publicized a new list of cooperation partners. A total of 310 central departments and institutions appeared on the list, and for the first time the 592 poor counties were all paired up with partners.

The assistance may be provided by way of projects, economic development, creating enterprises, and paired-up assistance:

(1) Assistance projects suited to local conditions. For instance, the Ministry of Water Resources has assigned money to six

目帮扶为主的扶贫工作，采取“项目扶持、资金支持”的方式，实施以“六大工程”建设为重点的民生水利工程，解决当地的基础设施、农田水利、村容村貌、教育等问题，扶贫成效明显。

其二，以产业开发为着力点的定点扶贫模式。这种模式以产业开发为重点，通过促进当地产业结构改善，带动地区经济发展，提高农民发展能力，实现落后地区的可持续发展，解决贫困问题。科技部在光山、佳县、井冈山、永新、魏县、英山、柞水等定点帮扶县，整合科技资源，聚焦关键技术攻关，重视科技示范作用，指导各地科技扶贫工作，促进了贫困地区特色产业发展。

其三，以企业发展为推手的定点扶贫模式。这种模式以扶持贫困地区的龙头企业为引领，带动地区经济发展，转移农业劳动力，解决贫困问题。该模式以中国石油天然气集团公司定点帮扶台前县为典型代表。2007年，中国石油天然气集团公司承接河南省台前县定点扶贫任务，发挥石油石化行业优势，扶持当地龙头企业——濮阳市恒润石化公司，带动当地石油石化产业发展，促进经济增长和农民增收。

其四，以结对帮扶为手段的扶贫模式。在中央、省级部门的扶贫推动与宏观

projects in its paired counties, which have substantially improved local infrastructure, farmland irrigation, water conservancy, village conditions, and education;

(2) Economic development for sustainable growth of underdeveloped regions through improving the local industrial structure, boosting the regional economy, and enhancing the farmers' capacity for development. The Ministry of Science and Technology has provided technological assistance to its paired counties of Guangshan, Jiaxian, Jinggangshan, Yongxin, Weixian, Yingshan and Zhashui, thus promoting specialized industrial development in these places;

(3) Developing businesses to create jobs and drive the local economy. For example PetroChina was assigned to help Taiqian County of Henan Province in 2007. It has since supported Hengrun in Puyang, a leading local petrochemical plant, and consequently boosted the local oil and petrochemical industries and brought more income to local farmers; and

(4) Paired-up assistance for targeted effects. City and county governments in impoverished areas have developed modes

指导下，贫困地区的市、县级政府积极响应国家的号召，探索了诸如“对口帮扶”“结对助困”等适合本地区特点的社会扶贫发展模式。例如，陕西省榆林府谷县创造了“3331”的扶贫方式。即利用3年时间，每年至少帮扶3000户，做到帮扶到村、到户、到人“三到位”，实现全县贫困人口整体脱贫这一目标。

of paired-up social assistance to suit local poverty alleviation. For instance, Fugu County in Shaanxi Province has adopted a "3331" model: designating local officials to help at least 3,000 households a year and provide assistance to every village, every household and every villager in order to realize the one goal of poverty elimination in three years through paired-up assistance.

社会扶贫

社会扶贫是指多元行动主体针对贫困人口和社会弱势群体所提供的各种救助、开发以及社会服务活动。自20世纪90年代中期开始，社会扶贫一直是中国扶贫的重要组成部分。中国的社会扶贫是具有中国特色的广义的社会扶贫概念，大体可划分为三种主要类型：第一种是政府组织和协调的带有再分配性质的社会扶贫，包括各级机关事业单位开展的定点扶贫、东西协作扶贫以及军队和武警部队扶贫；第二种是企业基于社会责任，开展与贫困地区互利的企业扶贫；第三种是以非营利性的社会组织和个人为主进行的纯粹的扶贫活动。这三种方式构成的社会扶贫，为中国减贫事业作出了重要的贡献。

社会扶贫作为一种具有中国特色的扶贫模式，有着自身独特的理论、实践及政策背景，与专项扶贫、行业扶贫共同构成中国扶贫开发的大扶贫格局。

Social Assistance in Poverty Alleviation

Social assistance refers to all kinds of aid, development help and social services provided by multiple actors to poor population and disadvantaged groups. Social assistance has since the mid-1990s been an important part of China's poverty alleviation campaign.

Social assistance can be generally divided into three types:

(1) Redistribution under government organization and coordination, including designated tasks undertaken by Party and government departments at all levels, cooperation between the east and the west, and missions performed by the military and armed police force;

(2) Corporate involvement to fulfill their social responsibility for helping poor areas; and

(3) Pure assistance offered by non-profit social organizations and individuals.

These three types of social assistance each make a great contribution to China's poverty reduction efforts. Together with special programs and corporate support, they form great synergy in the all-encompassing campaign against poverty.

东西部扶贫协作

东西部扶贫协作，即东部发达省市与西部贫困地区结对开展扶贫协作，是国家为实现共同富裕目标作出的一项制度性安排。自1996年开始，经过几次调整和变动，东西部扶贫协作已形成目前9省（市）、5个计划单列市和4个大城市对口帮扶西部10个省（区、市）的工作格局。东西部扶贫协作形式多样，形成了以政府援助、企业合作、社会帮扶、人才支持为主的基本工作框架。

实施东西部扶贫协作工作以来，东部发达省份与西部贫困地区在结对治理贫困的具体实践中不断探索扶贫方式与模式，具体有：基于企业合作层面的扶贫模式、创建高层沟通机制的扶贫模式、选择贫困重点的扶贫模式。

其一，基于企业合作层面的东西部扶贫协作模式。指通过推动东西部地区的企业合作，带动贫困地区企业的发展，增强贫困地区的市场活力，提高贫困地区劳动力素质，解决落后地区的贫困问题。比如，山东省的14个地级市结对帮扶重庆市的14个国家扶贫开发工作重点县，在企业

East-West Cooperation in Poverty Alleviation

This refers to the practice of pairing the developed provinces and municipalities in the east with the impoverished regions in the west. It is a policy to reduce poverty and achieve common prosperity.

After several adjustments since 1996, nine provinces (municipalities), five cities that enjoy provincial-level status in the state economic plan, and four major cities in east China have been paired with 10 provinces, autonomous regions and municipality in west China. Cooperation in diverse forms has continued, and a working framework has been built with government backing, cooperation from enterprises, social assistance, and human resources support.

Under this framework the east and the west have explored effective ways of cooperation, creating three successful models:

(1) east-west cooperation between enterprises. This drives the growth of enterprises in poor areas, increases market vigor, and improves the ability of the local workforce to fight poverty in backward areas. For instance, 14 prefecture-level cities of Shandong Province in east China have partnered with 14 key poor counties of Chongqing Municipality in west

合作的基础上，争取政府援助。同时，积极开展社会帮扶，推动社会力量参与扶贫。

其二，创建高层沟通机制的东西部扶贫协作模式。指东西部扶贫协作双方创建与坚持有效的沟通交流机制。比如，1996年至2019年，福建省与宁夏回族自治区每年召开一次联席会议，确保闽宁协作中的大方针和大方向，保证双方及时获取需要的信息，交流学习先进管理理念。双方通过加强省到各区县各层级的对接，提高了沟通的时效性。

其三，集中于重点贫困地区的东西部扶贫协作模式。指将贫困地区中贫困程度更深的地区作为扶贫重点的扶贫方式。比如，2010年，根据内蒙古自治区乌兰察布市、赤峰市两地经济社会发展滞后、贫困面大、贫困面深的实际情况，京蒙扶贫协作作出了调整：由原来帮扶8个盟市调整为重点帮扶乌兰察布市与赤峰市各8个旗（县、市）。

东西部扶贫协作有力推动了“西部大开发”战略的实施，为减贫事业作出了巨大贡献。在扶贫开发实践中，形成了一些成功的经验：一是建立扶贫协作双方的长期沟通与交流机制，这是双方开展扶贫工作的前提；二是重视企业合作，企业的发展能迅速而有效地激活贫困地区的市场活

China. In addition to cooperation between enterprises, these cities in Shandong also seek government assistance and invite public participation in the poverty alleviation initiative;

(2) a high-level communication mechanism for east-west cooperation. For instance, since 1996 Fujian Province in southeast China and Ningxia Hui Autonomous Region in northwest China have held annual joint meetings to discuss the focus and principles for bilateral cooperation, and exchange information and management expertise. This interaction enhances timely communication; and

(3) east-west cooperation focusing on key areas of extreme poverty. For instance, in 2010, Beijing adjusted its assistance to Inner Mongolia Autonomous Region, from previously assisting eight of the latter's leagues and cities to assisting eight banners (counties and cities) in each of the Ulanqab League and Chifeng City, as these two places suffer extensive and serious poverty and an underdeveloped economy.

East-west cooperation has substantially promoted China's large-scale development of the western region, and greatly contributed to poverty reduction there. Successful experiments include:

(1) Long-term mechanisms that facilitate communication and exchanges between east and west partners;

(2) Enterprises are swift and effective in cooperation to stimulate market vigor in poor

力，发展贫困地区经济；三是注重人才交流，人才是贫困地区可持续发展的保障。

areas and develop the local economy; and

(3) Exchanges of human resources support the sustainable development of poor areas.

坚持从严要求，促进真抓实干

Strict Standards for Practical Progress

底线任务

中共十八大以来，习近平多次强调，要善于运用底线思维的方法。底线思维是以底线为导向的一种思维方法和心态，要求不回避矛盾，不掩盖不足，客观分析每个可能出现的问题，并妥善加以解决。

这一思维方法也体现在习近平关于扶贫工作的重要论述之中。他指出，农村贫困人口如期脱贫、贫困县全部摘帽、解决区域性整体贫困，是全面建成小康社会的底线任务，是中国共产党作出的庄严承诺。没有农村贫困人口全部脱贫，就没有全面建成小康社会，这个底线任务不能打任何折扣，党向人民作出的承诺不能打任何折扣。

中共十八大以来，中共中央把贫困人口脱贫作为全面建成小康社会的底线任务和标志性指标，在全国范围全面打响了脱贫攻坚战。脱贫攻坚作为“底线任务”，不仅意味着要保质（“两不愁三保障”）保量（农村贫困人口全部脱贫）完成，还意味着脱贫攻坚作为全面建成小康社会“补短板”的关键任务，必须如期完成。

Bottom-Line Tasks for Achieving Moderate Prosperity

"Bottom-line thinking" is a way of thinking based on objective analysis of problems for proper solution, rather than blinding oneself to them or ignoring potential risks.

Xi advocates such an approach to poverty alleviation. He calls the goals of China's poverty elimination – to help the rural population eliminate poverty as scheduled, lift all poor counties out of poverty and solve overall regional poverty – "a bottom-line task" in building a moderately prosperous society in all respects. It is also a solemn promise made by the Party. China cannot say that it has achieved this objective if its rural poor have not all been lifted out of poverty. This task must be fulfilled to the letter, and the Party's promise to the people must be honored in full.

Since 2012, the CPC Central Committee has taken this task as a symbol of building China into a society of moderate prosperity. It must be fulfilled as scheduled both in "quality" (assuring those living in poverty of adequate food and clothing and guaranteeing their access to compulsory education, basic medical services and safe housing) and in "quantity" (lifting all out of poverty).

“扶真贫、真扶贫”

习近平多次在不同场合强调，新时代的脱贫攻坚就是要做到“扶真贫、真扶贫”，这充分表明党中央打赢脱贫攻坚战的决心和信心，同时表明了中央对于脱贫攻坚从严要求、促进真抓实干的态度。

“扶真贫”，指脱贫攻坚要保证将真正贫困的人口纳入到扶贫对象之中，并且扶贫对象中不存在非贫困人口，同时也要保证真正贫困的农村人口全部被纳入到贫困人口建档立卡之中，不存在部分甚至是极少数的贫困人口被排斥于扶贫对象框定之外的情况。

“真扶贫”，指对“精准帮扶”进行考核评估，监督政府、社会等各类扶贫资源是否较为顺畅且完整地传递给扶贫对象，保证扶贫措施与贫困识别结果实现有效衔接，扶贫资金使用安排能够很好地满足不同类型贫困农户的脱贫致富需求，扶贫资金使用达到较高效益水平。对此，习近平指出，扶贫工作必须务实，脱贫过程必须扎实，扶真贫、真扶贫，脱贫结果必须真

Helping Those in Need and Delivering Genuine Outcomes

Xi Jinping demands that poverty elimination in the new era must reach those who truly need it and deliver genuine outcomes. This shows the central leadership's commitment, confidence and resolution in winning the battle against poverty.

By "reaching those who truly need it," all of those who are genuinely poor will be registered as living in poverty and identified as the recipients of assistance, and all false claimants will be excluded.

By "delivering genuine outcomes," examinations and reviews of relevant assistance will be conducted to ensure that government and social assistance resources are delivered to the eligible recipients smoothly and in full, that relief measures and poverty identification are well integrated, and that relief funds are used in an effective way to meet the needs of different households.

Xi Jinping instructs that poverty elimination work must be down-to-earth, progress must be steady, and results must be real. The results

实，让脱贫成效真正获得群众认可、经得起实践和历史检验，决不搞花拳绣腿，决不摆花架子。

must be accepted by the people and must withstand the test of time. Acting purely for show is forbidden.

提高脱贫质量

脱贫攻坚规定了扶贫对象的量化脱贫标准，“一达标、两不愁、三保障”。但是，容易被忽视的是，单纯地套用脱贫标准来评价是否脱贫容易导致数字脱贫、虚假脱贫现象。脱贫质量的概念由此应运而生，其意义是让脱贫标准回归真正脱贫的内涵。在某种意义上，可以说脱贫质量是完整版的脱贫标准，内涵包括结果真实、稳定脱贫、效益良好和程序规范四个方面。

对此，习近平指出，脱贫既要看数量，更要看质量，不能到时候都说完成了脱贫任务，过一两年又大规模返贫。要多管齐下提高脱贫质量，巩固脱贫成果。要严把贫困退出关，严格执行退出的标准和程序，确保脱真贫、真脱贫。要把防止返贫摆在重要位置，适时组织对脱贫人口开展“回头看”，对返贫人口和新发生贫困人口及时予以帮扶。要探索建立稳定脱贫长效机制，强化产业扶贫，组织消费扶贫，加大培训力度，促进转移就业，让贫困群众有稳定的工作岗位。要做好易地扶贫搬迁后续帮扶。要加强扶贫同扶志扶智相结合，让脱贫具有可持续的内生动力。

Enhancing the Effectiveness of Poverty Elimination

China has set clear standards for poverty elimination. But if these standards are simplistically applied in evaluating the results, it may lead to fake poverty elimination or being apparent only in figures. So the effectiveness of poverty elimination must be ensured, with outcomes, stability, effects and procedures all taken into consideration.

Xi Jinping emphasizes the need for both "quality" and "quantity." It will be a failure if poverty is reportedly eliminated, but within one or two years the people return to poverty again. Progress must be demonstrable, and evaluation of the results must follow strict criteria in accordance with strict procedures.

To prevent people from returning to poverty, follow-up checks at appropriate intervals will be conducted, and timely assistance provided to those newly caught in poverty or returning to poverty. A long-term mechanism for stable poverty elimination will be built to support local business development, boost consumption of local products and services, provide training, and create stable jobs for the poor. Follow-up assistance will continue after relocation, and the poor will acquire necessary skills to escape poverty with more confidence, so that poverty elimination will be sustained through their internal impetus.

干部轮训

精准扶贫不仅要使广大贫困群众早日精准脱贫，更要在精准扶贫的实践中培养和锻炼各级干部，改善基层治理。习近平曾对脱贫攻坚工作作出重要指示:“基层一线扶贫工作者是脱贫攻坚的生力军，对他们要在政治上关心、工作上支持、生活上保障，支持他们在脱贫攻坚战场上奋发有为、大显身手。”干部扶贫培训正是支持扶贫工作者奋发作为的重要途径，一条标本兼顾的干部培养道路，是如期打赢脱贫攻坚战的现实需要，同样也是国家治理体系现代化的需要。

为此，要突出抓好各级扶贫干部的学习培训。对县级以上领导干部，重点是提高思想认识，引导树立正确政绩观，掌握精准脱贫方法论，培养研究攻坚问题、解决攻坚难题的能力。对基层干部，重点是提高实际能力，培育懂扶贫、会帮扶、作风硬的扶贫干部队伍。要吸引各类人才参与脱贫攻坚和农村发展，关心爱护基层一线扶贫干部，激励他们为打好脱贫攻坚战努力工作。

Rotation Training of Officials

While providing assistance to the poor, targeted poverty alleviation also offers a broad arena to test officials at all levels and improve community governance.

Xi Jinping has stated, "The frontline workers in the battle against poverty are the main forces. We should give them political care, support their work, guarantee their living conditions, and encourage them to distinguish themselves on the front line." Training is a way to give them great support. Training is also needed to ensure victory over poverty and to modernize China's state governance.

To this end, training must be well designed and well organized. Officials at county level and above will be guided to raise their theoretical understanding, foster a correct view of performance, learn to apply the methods of targeted poverty elimination, and increase their capacity for analyzing and tackling difficult problems. Community workers must improve their skills so that they understand poverty alleviation well, are able to offer proper assistance, and are strongly disciplined. More people will be encouraged to engage in poverty elimination and rural development, and community workers will receive good care and be motivated to work hard at the front line.

脱贫攻坚责任书

建立精准扶贫工作机制是多部门参与、协同推进的系统工程。中共十八大以来，精准扶贫考核机制在党的统一领导和决策部署下不断完善，尤其是22个中西部省区市的一把手与中央签订《脱贫攻坚责任书》，立下“军令状”，实现了有史以来最严格的考核督查问责机制。

2015年6月18日，习近平在贵州召开部分省区市党委主要负责同志座谈会时强调，各级党委和政府要确保贫困人口到2020年如期脱贫。要实现2020年如期脱贫，全体人民共同迈入全面小康社会的一个重要推手就是创新精准扶贫考核机制。为落实各层级部门扶贫责任，中央出台精准扶贫责任制实施办法，强化“中央统筹、省负总责、市县抓落实”的扶贫管理体制机制，构建起责任清晰、各负其责、合力攻坚的责任体系。目前，就有关考核机制创新，各级政府层层签订脱贫攻坚责任书，建立年度脱贫攻坚报告和督察制度，把脱

Poverty Elimination Pledges

Since 2012, the mechanism for evaluating targeted poverty alleviation has been improved under the CPC leadership. The top officials of the 22 provinces, autonomous regions and municipality in central and western China have made poverty elimination pledges to the central leadership. This is the strictest evaluation and supervision ever practiced to enhance accountability.

When talking to a meeting of senior officials of some provinces, autonomous regions and a municipality held in Guizhou on June 18, 2015, Xi Jinping demanded that Party committees and governments at all levels must ensure elimination of poverty within their respective jurisdiction by 2020 as planned. For this purpose, a new evaluation mechanism is needed so that officials at all levels will take on specific duties. A poverty alleviation working mechanism is now in place, whereby the central leadership makes overall plans, provincial authorities take overall responsibility, and city and county authorities are responsible for implementation, with a clear division of responsibilities and coordination of the endeavors of the various parties.

To date, local governments have all signed pledges and now make annual reports

贫攻坚实绩作为选拔任用干部的重要依据，激励各级干部到脱贫攻坚战场上大显身手，为2020年如期脱贫提供了重要保障。

under a supervision system for poverty elimination. The officials are encouraged to distinguish themselves in the battle against poverty, and their performance will be a major criterion for promotion.

中央统筹、省负总责、市县抓落实

脱贫攻坚战建立了分工明确、体系严谨的领导责任制，为各层级、各部门参与脱贫攻坚建立了基础性的工作机制。2015年6月，习近平要求强化扶贫开发工作领导责任制，把中央统筹、省负总责、市（地）县抓落实的管理体制落到实处。2015年11月，《中共中央 国务院关于打赢脱贫攻坚战的决定》要求“强化脱贫攻坚领导责任制”。2016年10月，中共中央办公厅、国务院办公厅印发《脱贫攻坚责任制实施办法》。由此，脱贫攻坚“中央统筹、省负总责、市县抓落实”的领导责任制基本形成，并在不断完善中为打赢脱贫攻坚战提供坚实保障。

在这一体制下，中共中央、国务院主要负责统筹制定扶贫开发大政方针，出台重大政策举措，规划重大工程项目。省（自治区、直辖市）党委和政府对扶贫开发工作负总责，需要结合省情，抓好目标

A Mechanism of Defined Responsibilities

China has established a system of leadership with clearly defined responsibilities for officials at different levels to ensure victory over poverty.

Xi Jinping in June 2015 instructed that the system for leadership responsibilities in poverty alleviation and development be reinforced, whereby the central leadership makes overall plans, provincial authorities take overall responsibility, and city and county authorities take charge of implementation. The Decision on Winning the Battle Against Poverty, in November 2015, made a similar requirement. In October 2016, the central authorities released the Regulations on Poverty Alleviation Responsibilities, marking the formalization of the said leadership system.

Under this system, the CPC Central Committee and the State Council are responsible for formulating major principles, strategies, policies and measures, and devising major projects. The Party committees and governments of provinces, autonomous regions and municipalities take overall responsibility for development-oriented poverty alleviation, and based on local conditions, they will set goals, assign projects, allocate funds, mobilize the

确定、项目下达、资金投放、组织动员、监督考核等工作。市（地）党委和政府的主要职责在于做好上下衔接、域内协调、督促检查工作，把精力集中在贫困县如期摘帽上。县级党委和政府承担主体责任，书记和县长是第一责任人，需要结合县域实际，做好进度安排、项目落地、资金使用、人力调配、推进实施等工作。

public, and supervise and evaluate relevant implementation. The Party committees and governments of cities (prefectures) are responsible for coordinating the work as a major link between higher authorities and counties at lower levels in their respective jurisdictions, and scrutinizing relevant work and progress. Their primary task is to ensure their poor counties escape poverty as scheduled. The Party committees and governments of counties take on the duties as major actors in poverty alleviation, and their Party secretaries and mayors are to assume main responsibility for the work. Based on the conditions in their counties, they set the schedule, make good use of funds, coordinate labor distribution, and urge progress in relevant work and projects.

“绣花”功夫

“绣花”功夫是习近平关于如何坚持精准方略、如何提高脱贫实效的生动比喻，在他看来，解决好“扶持谁、谁来扶、怎么扶、如何退”四个问题，全过程都要精准，有的甚至需要下一番“绣花”功夫。扶贫不是定了贫困户以后给他们几头羊、几袋种子，给他们盖房子或者搬走了事，而是要针对不同贫困户，帮助其解决不同的致贫原因。

根据精准扶贫精准脱贫的基本方略以及习近平的相关论述，可以从以下两个方面理解“绣花”的含义：一是扶贫政策要细化，要在具体的实践中做“细活”。习近平指出：“扶贫是大政策，大政策还要细化，就像绣花一样。”各地要按照中央关于脱贫攻坚的一系列顶层设计，根据地区发展情况，将有关政策做实做细。这就需要像“绣花”一样，一丝不苟地将具体的扶贫工作做精准。二是扶贫政策要有针对性，要因地制宜、分类施策。他指出，不同的地方、不同的贫困户有不同的扶法。

"Being Meticulous Like Doing Embroidery"

"Being meticulous like doing embroidery" is a metaphor used by Xi Jinping for advancing efficient targeted poverty elimination. He calls for meticulous work at every stage in the whole process of poverty alleviation. Poverty alleviation does not simply mean handing out one or two goats or bags of grain seeds to poor households, building houses for them, or having them relocated elsewhere. Rather, it means identifying the root causes of poverty and helping poor households tackle them.

The requirement of "being meticulous like doing embroidery" has two implications:

(1) Policies must be detailed and well thought out so that they will be applicable under local conditions.

(2) Policies must be targeted for different localities and households. Overflowing

贫有百样、困有千种，大水漫灌式扶贫很难奏效，必须采取更精准的措施。这意味着精准扶贫也需要像绣花一样，根据不同的图案，使用不同的绣线和技法。

measures will not work to meet diverse needs. This is like an embroidery worker applying different techniques and choosing threads of different colors for different designs.

阳光扶贫

习近平指出，扶贫资金是贫困群众的“救命钱”，一分一厘都不能乱花，更容不得动手脚、玩猫腻。要加强扶贫资金阳光化管理，加强审计监管，集中整治和查处扶贫领域的职务犯罪，对挤占挪用、层层截留、虚报冒领、挥霍浪费扶贫资金的，要从严惩处。

扶贫开发同样是资源配置过程。如何避免形式主义的假扶贫，减少扶贫资源的“跑冒滴漏”，一直是一个世界性难题。一方面，地方政府及相关组织作为扶贫政策的执行工具有自利倾向，会造成扶贫资源的浪费；另一方面，政策执行的信息不对称也会造成政策的消极执行。对此，习近平提出了“廉洁扶贫、阳光扶贫”，要求加大对各级干部扶贫工作的考核力度。

其中，阳光扶贫的要求是：扶贫工作始终把纪律和规矩挺在前面，不断完善制度，加强监管，坚决惩治和预防扶贫领域违纪违法行为。要完善扶贫资金项目公告公示制度，建立健全贫困群众全程参与脱

Transparency in Poverty Alleviation

Funds for poverty relief are intended to help those in need, and it is unacceptable that a single coin might be wasted or misused. There will be transparent management and strict auditing, and work-related crimes in poverty alleviation will be investigated and punished. Those who dare to misappropriate, retain, falsely claim, or squander poverty relief funds will be severely punished.

Development-oriented poverty alleviation is a matter of distribution of resources. Avoiding malpractice and plugging loopholes have remained a problem around the world. On the one hand, local governments and other organizations as the executors of relevant policies might try to use policies to benefit themselves first, thereby leading to waste of relief resources; on the other, asymmetric information can easily lead to passive execution of policies. To tackle these problems, Xi Jinping demands "clean conduct and transparency in poverty alleviation" and strict evaluation of the officials involved.

To increase transparency, discipline and rules will be strictly observed, with improved institutions, strict scrutiny, and effective prevention and penalties for violations. Public notification of the application of poverty relief funds and projects will be improved, as will

贫攻坚的每一个步骤，发挥媒体监督、交叉考核监督、第三方评估的作用，确保扶贫资金使用、扶贫项目实施、脱贫验收过程公开透明，切实做到阳光化管理。

the procedures for the poor to participate in every step of poverty alleviation. Media scrutiny, cross-reviews and supervision between provinces, and third party evaluation will also be introduced and encouraged to enhance the transparent usage of funds, project implementation, and evaluation of relevant outcomes.

第三方评估机制

精准扶贫以来，各地积极引入第三方评估机制全面开展各项考核。2015年，《中共中央 国务院关于打赢脱贫攻坚战的决定》明确要求"建立对扶贫政策落实情况和扶贫成效的第三方评估机制"。

第三方评估是客观评判省级党委和政府扶贫开发工作精准度、群众满意度的重要依据。充分发挥第三方评估的督查、巡察作用，可为科学转变扶贫工作方式，消除贫困地区体制机制障碍，增强其内生动力与发展活力开辟有效途径。

中共十八大以来，为了加强脱贫攻坚成效考核，中央开始实行最严格的考核评估制度。国务院扶贫办2016年、2017年组织了由中国科学院牵头的第三方评估，选派相关专家学者进村入户，对各地贫困人口的识别精准度、贫困人口退出的精准度和贫困人口对帮扶工作的满意度进行第三方评估，起到查实问题、总结经验、以评促改、支撑决策的作用。中科院地理科学与资源研究所还研究制定了《贫困县脱贫退出第三方评估技术指南》，就调研流程、协调部署、应急处理等开展专门培训，统一规范调查问卷类型、内容、填

Third Party Evaluation

As required by the Decision on Winning the Battle Against Poverty, third party evaluation has been introduced to review the execution of poverty alleviation policies and the results of poverty alleviation endeavors.

Third party evaluation provides an objective reference for assessing the precision of the work done by provincial Party committees and governments, and the satisfaction of the general public. This is an effective way to improve relevant work, remove institutional obstacles, and impart vigor to poor regions.

Since 2012, the central authorities have introduced the strictest-ever system for review and evaluation of poverty elimination. The State Council Leading Group Office of Poverty Alleviation and Development in 2016 and 2017 organized third party evaluation headed by the Chinese Academy of Sciences (CAS). Experts and academics visited poor villages and households to obtain accurate information on identifying and eliminating poverty, and on paired-up assistance. Their research helped identify problems, summarize experience, urge improvement and support decision-making.

The CAS researchers also formulated a Technical Guide to Third Party Evaluation of Poverty Elimination in Poor Counties. They conducted training on research procedures,

写、记录、编码、数据处理等问题，在保证各项工作的技术性、专业性、细致性的基础上，构建独立公正的精准扶贫考核机制。引入第三方评估之后，由社会专业组织作为独立的第三方对于扶贫脱贫工作进行客观评估，既丰富了评估的方式，也使得评估更加有效。

work coordination and emergency response, and created standard questionnaires with clear rules for the content, filling, recording, coding and data processing. Based on these, an independent and fair evaluation mechanism has been built.

Inviting specialist organizations as independent third parties to evaluate poverty elimination enhances the effects of the evaluation.

扶贫领域腐败和作风问题专项治理

中共十九届中央纪委坚决贯彻习近平的指示批示要求和中共中央决策部署，高度重视扶贫领域腐败和作风问题专项治理，把专项治理工作摆上重要日程。中央纪委决定从2018年到2020年，在全国开展扶贫领域的腐败和作风问题的专项治理，国务院扶贫开发领导小组也把2018年作为扶贫领域作风建设年。为此，中央纪委和国务院扶贫开发领导小组都制定了工作方案，进行了具体的工作部署，以重点解决两个方面的问题。一是“四个意识”不强，没有把脱贫攻坚摆在应有的位置。二是不够精准，工作落实不到位，考核评估不严肃、不严格。中央纪委和各地各部门坚持以上率下，深入基层调研督导，有效扎实推动工作，形成了主要领导亲自抓、分管领导具体抓、上下联动深入抓的工作格局，取得了初步成效。

Rectification of Corruption and Misconduct in Poverty Alleviation

Following the instructions of Xi Jinping and the plans of the CPC Central Committee, the 19th Central Commission for Discipline Inspection has been conducting a special nationwide campaign, from 2018 to 2020, to rectify corruption and address misconduct related to poverty alleviation. The State Council Leading Group Office of Poverty Alleviation and Development made 2018 the year for improving conduct in poverty alleviation.

These two organizations have devised specific work plans to tackle problems in two respects: One is a weak understanding of the "Four Consciousnesses" and insufficient weight given to poverty alleviation; the other is that measures taken are neither properly targeted nor fully applied, and the review of related work is lenient. The chief officials and others in charge of discipline inspection have all been involved in this rectification, conducting investigations and directing the work top-down with initial effects.

最严格的考核评估

为确保脱贫成效经得起实践、人民、历史检验，中共中央明确要求实行最严格的考核评估制度。近年来，以国务院扶贫办为核心的主要扶贫单位相继实行了严格的考核制度，确保贫困人口享受到扶贫政策。尤其是在脱贫攻坚考核评估方面，开展了包括国家有关部门的考核、省际之间的交叉考核、委托科研机构进行的第三方评估考核等。

中共中央办公厅、国务院办公厅2016年2月印发了《省级党委和政府扶贫开发工作成效考核办法》，提出将考核结果作为对省级党委、政府主要负责人和领导班子综合考核评价的重要依据。

《办法》旨在确保到2020年现行标准下农村贫困人口实现脱贫，贫困县全部摘帽，解决区域性整体贫困，适用于中西部22个省（自治区、直辖市）党委和政府扶贫开发工作成效的考核。《办法》明确，考核工作从2016年到2020年，每年开展一次，由国务院扶贫开发领导小组组织进行，具体工作由国务院扶贫办、中央组织

Strictest Review and Evaluation of Poverty Elimination

China has introduced the strictest system for review and evaluation to ensure that poverty elimination policies reach the poor and the results stand the tests of practice, the people and history. Reviews conducted by government departments, cross-reviews between provinces, and third party evaluations by scientific research institutions have been carried out.

In February 2016 the central authorities issued the Methods for Evaluating the Performances of Provincial Party Committees and Governments in Poverty Alleviation and Development, making the evaluation results a major criterion for overall assessment of provincial-level leaderships.

The document applies to the 22 provinces, autonomous regions and municipality in central and western China to ensure that the three goals for 2020 are fulfilled: helping all rural population living under current poverty line escape poverty, eliminating poverty in all poor countries, and eliminating overall regional poverty. The State Council Leading Group of Poverty Alleviation and Development is in charge of organizing annual evaluations from 2016 to 2020, which are conducted by its member units

部牵头，会同国务院扶贫开发领导小组成员单位组织实施。

根据《办法》，考核内容包括：（1）减贫成效。考核贫困人口数量减少、贫困县退出、贫困地区农村居民收入增长情况。（2）精准识别。考核贫困人口识别、退出精准度。（3）精准帮扶。考核对驻村工作队和帮扶责任人帮扶工作的满意度。（4）扶贫资金。依据财政专项扶贫资金绩效考评办法，重点考核各省（自治区、直辖市）扶贫资金安排、使用、监管和成效等。

考核中发现下列问题的，由国务院扶贫开发领导小组提出处理意见：未完成年度减贫计划任务的；违反扶贫资金管理使用规定的；违反贫困县约束规定，发生禁止作为事项的；违反贫困退出规定，弄虚作假、搞“数字脱贫”的；贫困人口识别

headed by the Leading Group's office and the Department of Organization under the CPC Central Committee.

According to the document, the evaluation covers the following areas:

(1) Results of poverty reduction, reflected by a decrease in poor population, poverty elimination in poor counties, and increased incomes for rural residents in poor areas;

(2) Precise identification of the poor population and assessment of their escape from poverty;

(3) Precise assistance, reflected by the satisfaction of the resident work teams and staff designated for the assistance; and

(4) Assistance funds, reflected by the arrangement, usage, supervision and impact of the funds in provinces, autonomous regions and municipality.

The Leading Group will deal with the following problems:

- Failure to complete yearly poverty reduction tasks;
- Violations of relevant rules on the usage and management of relief funds;
- Violations of relevant prohibitions concerning poor counties;
- Fake poverty reduction or reduction apparent only in figures;
- Low accuracy in poverty identification and elimination;
- Low satisfaction of the people assisted; and
- Violations of other discipline and

和退出准确率、帮扶工作群众满意度较低的；存在纪检、监察、审计和社会监督发现违纪违规问题的。

《办法》明确，考核结果由国务院予以通报。对完成年度减贫计划成效显著的省份，给予一定奖励。对出现前述问题的，对省级党委、政府主要负责人进行约谈，提出限期整改要求；对情节严重、造成不良影响的，追究相应责任。

rules discovered by the disciplinary inspection, supervision and auditing authorities and by the public.

The results of the evaluation will be made public by the State Council. Provinces, autonomous regions and municipality will be rewarded for notably fulfilling the yearly poverty reduction plans. If the above-listed problems are found, the chief officials will be summoned and given a deadline to rectify the situation; and if there are serious problems and adverse consequences, the chief officials will be held accountable.

坚持群众主体，激发内生动力

Motivating the People as the Main Actors

开发式扶贫

开发式扶贫，是对传统的救济式扶贫的改革和调整，是中国政府扶贫政策的核心和基础。实行这个方针，就是以经济建设为中心，支持和鼓励贫困地区的干部、群众开发当地资源、发展商品生产、改善生产条件，增强自我积累、自我发展的能力。

坚持开发式扶贫是中国特色反贫困道路的重要特点，强调把发展作为解决贫困问题的根本途径，视贫困群众为扶贫开发的重要主体。中国不仅要减少贫困人口数量，还要提高贫困人口发展能力，促进贫困人口融入社会；不仅要帮助贫困人口摆脱贫困状态，还要降低人们陷入贫困的风险。开发式扶贫通过建构有利于农村产业发展的基础条件，引导贫困人口参与其中，不仅在经济意义上使贫困人口摆脱贫困，而且在社会层面使贫困人口远离贫困。

进入脱贫攻坚阶段，中国坚持开发式扶贫方针不动摇，动员和引导贫困群众将自己苦干巧干与党委、政府帮扶相结合，充分开发当地资源，逐步形成自我积累、自我发展能力，最终实现脱贫。随着贫困人口分布、贫困成因、贫困特征等情

Development-Oriented Poverty Alleviation

Development-oriented poverty alleviation is different from the previous approach of providing funds to the poor. It is China's core policy on poverty alleviation. Officials and residents in poor areas are encouraged to exploit local resources, expand commodity production, improve productive conditions, and increase their capacity for endogenous development.

It highlights development as the essential means to end poverty, and regards the poor as the main actors. China aims to reduce the size of poor population, enhance people's relevant skills and integrate them into wider society. In addition to lifting the poor out of poverty, it also works to lower the possibility of their becoming victims of poverty in the first place.

Development-oriented poverty alleviation produces the basic conditions for rural economic development, and guides the poor to enlist in the effort. This will help them escape poverty both economically and socially.

China is following this approach in the last stage of its battle against poverty. The people are being mobilized and encouraged

况的变化，党和政府不断调整完善扶贫策略和帮扶方式，更加强调扶贫的精准性。同时，还高度重视激发贫困群众的内生动力，充分调动贫困群众的积极性、主动性、创造性，教育和引导贫困群众依靠自己的辛勤劳动实现脱贫致富。

to work hard and apply their own ingenuity in addition to government support. They will fully exploit the local resources, make continual accumulation, and enhance development capacity for final poverty elimination. The CPC and the government will adjust the tactics and forms of assistance for targeted results in response to the changes in the distribution of poor population, and the causes and nature of their poverty. At the same time, efforts shall be made to ignite people's enthusiasm and creativeness, educate and guide them to shake off poverty with their own hard work.

内生动力

内生动力在最抽象意义上是指事物发展的内因，是个体和区域发展的根本力量。激发贫困群众、贫困地区脱贫与发展的内生动力不仅是打赢脱贫攻坚战的重要战略选择，有助于更好更快地取得脱贫攻坚的最终胜利，而且是促进贫困群众全面发展的必由之路。唯有贫困群众拥有了脱贫的积极性和主动性，他们才能在真正意义上摆脱贫困。

中共十八大以来，习近平在多个场合就脱贫要靠内生动力作出重要指示，强调要输血和造血相结合、内外结合发展、变要我发展为我要发展、扶贫先扶智、阻止贫困代际传递、重视干部群众的首创精神，等等。他尤其重视激发贫困人口的内生脱贫动力，在他看来，贫困地区发展要靠内生动力，如果只是凭空救济出一个新村，或简单改变村容村貌，但其内在活力不行，劳动力不能回流，没有经济上的持续来源，这个地方的下一步发展也还是存在问题。只要贫困地区干部群众有走出贫

Internal Impetus for Poverty Elimination

Internal impetus is the fundamental force driving the development of individuals and regions. Motivating the poor and stimulating poor regions is a strategic approach to the battle against poverty. Only by applying their own initiative can these people escape poverty in the true sense.

Since 2012, Xi Jinping has advocated motivating the poor through such ideas as "aiding people" and "making people aid themselves." He wants to change the mindset from "others want me to develop" to "I want to develop," improve education facilities for the poor, stop the intergenerational transmission of poverty, and give play to the creativity of local officials and residents.

Xi values the internal motivation of the poor. If assistance only brightens the image of a village, or creates a brand new village out of nothing for relocated people, these places will still lack social vigor, and workers will not come back to work there. Without a strong catalyst for sustainable economic growth, these localities will still face problems. But if the local people have the confidence and

困的志向和内生动力，有更加振奋的精神状态、更加扎实的工作作风，坚持自力更生、艰苦奋斗，就能够凝聚起打赢脱贫攻坚战的强大力量。

resolution to fight poverty, work diligently, and apply high moral standards, they will build a strong synergy in the fight against poverty.

扶贫同扶志扶智结合

治贫先治愚。只有把下一代的教育工作做好，特别是要注重山区贫困地区下一代的成长，才能实现“真脱贫”。下一代要过上好生活，首先要有文化，这样将来他们的发展就会完全不同。中国古人有“家贫子读书”的传统，搞好贫困地区的义务教育，不让这些孩子输在起跑线上，才是根本的扶贫之策。

扶贫必扶智。让贫困地区的孩子们接受良好教育，是扶贫开发的重要任务，也是阻断贫困代际传递的重要途径。中国已经采取了一系列措施，推动贫困地区教育事业加快发展、教师队伍素质能力不断提高，力求让贫困地区的每一个孩子都能接受良好教育，实现德智体美全面发展，成为社会有用之才。

脱贫攻坚既要扶智也要扶志，坚持群众主体，激发内生动力。干部和群众是脱贫攻坚的重要力量，贫困群众既是脱贫

Poverty Alleviation Through Increasing People's Confidence and Helping Them Acquire Knowledge and Skills

To end poverty, the first step is to end ignorance and illiteracy. Only by educating the younger generations properly, particularly those in poor and mountainous areas, can genuine outcomes be delivered in poverty elimination. A good education will also bring a better life and a brighter future for young people. The Chinese have a tradition of valuing education even when suffering financial difficulties. Providing a good education will ensure that children in poor regions will not be losers before the race has begun, and will uproot poverty once and for all. It is a very effective way to stop intergenerational transmission of poverty.

To this end, China has adopted measures to improve education and the quality of teachers in poor regions, so that every child there can achieve well-rounded development.

Poverty elimination needs to increase people's confidence and help them acquire necessary knowledge and skills. While being recipients of poverty relief assistance, the poor are also major actors and a key force

攻坚的对象，更是脱贫攻坚的主体和基础。中国的一条重要扶贫经验就是依靠人民群众，充分调动贫困群众的积极性、主动性、创造性，坚持扶贫和扶志扶智相结合，正确处理外部帮扶和贫困群众自身努力的关系，培育贫困群众自力更生实现脱贫致富的意识，培养贫困群众发展生产和务工经商的技能，组织、引导、支持贫困群众用自己的辛勤劳动实现脱贫致富，用人民群众的内生动力支撑脱贫攻坚。

in fighting poverty. One approach to poverty elimination in China is to rely on the people and mobilize them to take part in the initiative. Equipped with a sense of self-reliance, the people will have confidence in their own ability to escape poverty and achieve prosperity. They will also be helped to acquire the skills they need to find jobs or do business, in order to support themselves and assist China's poverty elimination campaign.

产业扶贫

产业扶贫是一种建立在扶植产业发展基础上的扶贫开发政策方法，相比一般的产业化发展，更加强调对贫困人群的目标瞄准性和特惠性，更加强调贫困家庭从产业发展中受益。中国农村减贫发展长期重视产业的重要作用，从《国家八七扶贫攻坚计划（1994—2000年）》，到《中国农村扶贫开发纲要（2011—2020年）》，再到《中共中央 国务院关于打赢脱贫攻坚战的决定》，均十分重视发展产业促进贫困地区群众增收的重要性。

打响脱贫攻坚战以来，中共中央制定贫困地区特色产业发展规划，针对产业脱贫出台专项政策：实施贫困村“一村一品”产业推进行动，扶持建设一批贫困人口参与度高的特色农业基地；加强贫困地区农民合作社和龙头企业培育，发挥其对贫困人口的组织和带动作用，强化其与贫困户

Poverty Alleviation Through Creating New Economic Activity

This is a special policy devised to support poor regions. It targets the poor, gives them preferential treatment, and emphasizes the need to focus on local development.

China has relied on this strategy to help the poor increase their incomes and to end poverty in rural areas. This can be seen in a number of documents, including the Seven-year Program for Lifting 80 Million People Out of Poverty (1994-2000), the Outline for Development-oriented Poverty Alleviation of China's Rural Areas (2011-2020), and the Decision on Winning the Battle Against Poverty.

To win the battle against poverty, the central leadership has worked out a plan for developing new economic activity in poor areas with a host of supporting policies:

- Every poor village is encouraged to develop one special product of its own, and special farming bases are formed to create jobs for the impoverished population;
- Local cooperatives involving farmers and leading enterprises are supported to act as the driving force, and strengthen their ties with poor households;

的利益联结机制；支持贫困地区发展农产品加工业，加快一二三产业融合发展，让贫困户更多分享农业全产业链和价值链增值收益；加大对贫困地区农产品品牌推介营销支持力度；依托贫困地区特有的自然人文资源，深入实施乡村旅游扶贫工程；科学合理有序开发贫困地区水电、煤炭、油气等资源，调整完善资源开发收益分配政策；探索水电利益共享机制，将从发电中提取的资金优先用于水库移民和库区后续发展；引导中央企业、民营企业分别设立贫困地区产业投资基金，采取市场化运作方式，投入到吸引企业到贫困地区从事资源开发、产业园区建设、新型城镇化发展，等等。

- Poor areas receive support in developing food processing, and accelerate the integrated growth of agriculture, industry and the tertiary sector so that poor households will benefit more from the appreciation earnings of complete industrial and value chains;
- Marketing and promotion of farm produce from poor areas will be reinforced;
- The natural and cultural potential of poor areas will be tapped to develop rural tourism;
- Local hydropower, coal, oil, gas and other resources will be developed in a rational and orderly way, and the policy on distributing the returns from resource development will be adjusted;
- A hydropower benefit sharing mechanism will be developed, and the profits produced by power generation will be first used for relocating residents from reservoir zones and for future development of these zones; and
- State-owned enterprises and private businesses will be guided to set up investment funds for industrial development in poor areas, and use the market to attract more people to join in the development of local resources, industrial parks and new cities and towns in poor areas.

光伏扶贫

光伏扶贫是资产收益扶贫的有效方式，是产业扶贫的有效途径。光伏发电清洁环保、技术可靠、收益稳定，既适合建设户用和村级小电站，也适合建设较大规模的集中式电站，还可以结合农业、林业开展多种“光伏+”应用。在光照资源条件较好的地区因地制宜开展光伏扶贫，既符合精准扶贫精准脱贫战略，又符合国家清洁低碳能源发展战略；既有利于扩大光伏发电市场，又有利于促进贫困人口稳收增收。

从各地的实践看，光伏扶贫主要有四种类型：（1）户用光伏发电扶贫。利用贫困户屋顶或院落空地建设3~5KW的发电系统，产权和收益均归贫困户所有。（2）村级光伏电站扶贫。以村集体为建设主体，利用村集体的土地建设100~300KW的小型电站，产权归村集体所有，收益由村集体、贫困户按比例分配。（3）光伏大棚扶贫。利用农业大棚等现代农业设施现有支架建设的光伏电站，产权归投资企业

Photovoltage Projects for Poverty Alleviation

Photovoltage (PV) projects have proved effective in China's poverty alleviation efforts. Supported by reliable technologies, such clean power projects can produce stable incomes for the poor and benefit local development. The necessary equipment can be easily installed in small solar stations run by households or villages, or in large solar plants. They can also provide power for agriculture and forestry.

PV projects are especially suitable in places with a lot of sunshine. This also fits with China's strategy of developing clean and low-carbon energies.

PV projects of varying scales can be flexed according to local conditions:

(1) 3-5KW solar facilities for household use can stand on rooftops or in the courtyards of rural households, with the property rights and incomes belonging to the households;

(2) 100-300KW solar installations for village use can be erected on collectively owned village land, with the property rights belonging to the village and the benefits shared by the village and poor households;

(3) PV plants based on greenhouses, with the property rights jointly owned by the investing enterprises and the poor households; and

和贫困户共有。（4）光伏地面电站扶贫。利用荒山荒坡建设10MW以上的大型地面光伏电站，产权归投资企业所有，之后企业捐赠一部分股权，由当地政府将这部分股权收益分配给贫困户。

(4) 10MW-plus PV plants can extend on unused mountain slopes, with the property rights owned by the investing enterprises, which will donate some shares from which the benefits will be distributed to poor households by the local government.

教育扶贫

新中国成立以来，党和国家十分重视发展教育事业，开展普及九年制义务教育、扫除青壮年文盲、均衡发展优质教育资源、精准帮扶贫困家庭子女等一系列教育扶贫措施和行动，对扶贫攻坚作出了卓越贡献。中共十八大以来，习近平围绕“全面建成小康社会”提出了一系列新思想、新论断、新要求，对扶贫工作作出了一系列重要部署，对教育扶贫提出了明确要求。2015年11月，习近平在中央扶贫开发工作会议上强调，教育是阻断贫困代际传递的治本之策，贫困地区教育事业是管长远的，必须下大力气抓好，扶贫既要富口袋，也要富脑袋。

根据《关于实施教育扶贫工程的意见》，基础教育主要解决贫困地区办学条件差、教育基础设施薄弱、优质师资队伍欠缺、教育经费不足等造成的基础教育办学质量不达标以及基础教育普及程度不达标等问题；职业教育要提高促进脱贫致富的能力，提高贫困地区贫困人群的自主发展

Poverty Alleviation Through Education

The CPC and the Chinese government attach high importance to education. They have endeavored to promote nine-year compulsory education, eliminate illiteracy among young people, create a balance in the quality of education resources, and provide targeted assistance to children from poor families.

Since 2012, Xi Jinping has put forward a series of new ideas and requirements on building a moderately prosperous society in all respects, including poverty alleviation through education. He told the Central Conference on Poverty Alleviation and Development in November 2015 that education is the best way to stop intergenerational transmission of poverty, and education is of far-reaching significance to poor areas and must be developed well. While increasing material wealth, efforts are also needed to enrich people's knowledge.

According to the Guidelines on Poverty Alleviation Through Education, jointly formulated by a number of ministries in 2013, different goals are set for basic, vocational and higher education. Basic education will address such problems as poor school conditions, bad infrastructure, and lack of good teachers and educational funds, so that

能力，发展贫困地区区域性经济，解决贫困地区“造血能力”不足等问题；高等教育一方面要与贫困地区的经济、产业、科技发展相结合，促进贫困地区产业结构升级，另一方面要通过“继续实施高校招生倾斜政策”，保障和增加贫困地区学生接受高等教育的机会。

local education will meet relevant standards and reach eligible children. Vocational education will enhance people's capacity for self-development in order to escape poverty, achieve prosperity, develop the regional economy, and help poor regions find ways to aid themselves. Higher education should play a role in promoting the economic, industrial and technological development of poor areas, and advance the upgrading of their industrial structure. Colleges and universities will also enroll more candidates from poor areas and ensure their access to higher education.

携手消除贫困，共建人类命运共同体

Joining Hands to End Poverty and Build a Global Community with a Shared Future

联合国千年发展目标

新千年开始之际，全世界的领导人在联合国制定了一份广泛的愿景，旨在从多个方面着手抗击贫困。这一愿景转化为8个千年发展目标，成为在新千年最初的15年中全世界的总体发展框架。

8项目标包括:（1）消灭极端贫穷和饥饿;（2）实现普及初等教育;（3）促进两性平等并赋予妇女权力;（4）降低儿童死亡率;（5）改善产妇保健;（6）与艾滋病、疟疾和其他疾病作斗争;（7）确保环境的可持续能力;（8）制订促进发展的全球伙伴关系。

经过中国政府、社会各界、贫困地区广大干部群众共同努力以及国际社会积极帮助，中国7亿多农村贫困人口摆脱贫困。2015年，联合国千年发展目标在中国基本实现。中国是全球最早实现千年发展目标中减贫目标的发展中国家，为全球减贫事业作出了重大贡献。

Millennium Development Goals

At the start of this millennium, world leaders framed a wide-ranging vision at the United Nations, which was formulated as the Millennium Development Goals (MDGs), to be fulfilled by 2015.

There were eight goals:

(1) Eradicate extreme poverty and hunger;

(2) Achieve universal primary education;

(3) Promote gender equality and empower women;

(4) Reduce child mortality;

(5) Improve maternal health;

(6) Combat HIV/AIDS, malaria and other diseases;

(7) Ensure environmental sustainability; and

(8) Develop a global partnership for development.

With concerted efforts on the part of the Chinese government, social sectors and people in impoverished regions, and the international community, more than 70 million rural Chinese have been lifted out of poverty. By 2015, China had largely fulfilled the MDGs, becoming the first developing country to hit the target of reducing poverty ahead of the 2015 deadline and making an impressive contribution to global poverty reduction.

南南合作

由于世界上的发展中国家绝大部分都处于南半球和北半球的南部分，从20世纪60年代开始，这些国家之间为摆脱发达国家的控制，发展民族经济，开展专门的经济合作，形成了“南南合作”模式。中国是发展中国家的一员，是南南合作的积极倡导者和支持者。长期以来，中国本着“平等互利、注重实效、长期合作、共同发展”的原则，积极支持并参与南南合作。与发展中国家的合作已成为中国全方位对外开放战略的一部分，合作内容不断丰富，规模迅速扩大，形成经济上合作共赢局面。

习近平在2015减贫与发展高层论坛的主旨演讲中指出，消除贫困是人类的共同使命。中国在致力于自身消除贫困的同时，始终积极开展南南合作，力所能及向其他发展中国家提供不附加任何政治条件的援助，支持和帮助广大发展中国家特别是最不发达国家消除贫困。60多年来，中国共向166个国家和国际组织提供了近

South-South Cooperation

Most developing countries are located in the southern hemisphere or the southern part of the northern hemisphere. To escape control by developed countries and develop their own economy, these countries have since the 1960s engaged in economic cooperation among themselves, hence forming a South-South Cooperation model.

A developing country itself, China is an active advocate and supporter of South-South Cooperation. It participates in this cooperation under the principles of equality, mutual benefit and long-term cooperation for common development. Cooperation with other developing countries has been part of China's all-round opening up, with diverse projects on a growing scale.

In his keynote speech to the 2015 Global Poverty Reduction and Development Forum, Xi Jinping said that to eliminate poverty is the common mission of humanity. While working to eliminate domestic poverty, China is also committed to South-South Cooperation. It has provided assistance to other developing countries, to the best of its ability and with no political strings attached, and supported others, especially the least developed countries (LDCs), in eliminating poverty.

Over the past 60 years, China has provided nearly 400 billion yuan (US$63 billion) in aid to 166 countries and international

4000亿元人民币援助，派遣60多万援助人员，其中700多名中华好儿女为他国发展献出了宝贵生命。中国先后7次宣布无条件免除重债穷国和最不发达国家对华到期政府无息贷款债务，积极向亚洲、非洲、拉丁美洲和加勒比地区、大洋洲的69个国家提供医疗援助，先后为120多个发展中国家落实千年发展目标提供帮助。

中国坚定不移支持发展中国家消除贫困，推动更大范围、更高水平、更深层次的区域合作，通过对接发展战略，推进工业、农业、人力资源开发、绿色能源、环保等各领域务实合作，帮助各发展中国家把资源优势转化为发展优势。

organizations, and dispatched 600,000 workers on assistance missions, 700 of whom have scarified their lives in aiding developing countries. China has canceled inter-governmental interest-free loans owed by heavily-indebted poor countries and LDCs on seven occasions, provided medical support to 69 countries in Asia, Africa, Latin America, the Caribbean and Oceania, and helped more than 120 developing countries in fulfilling their MDGs.

China promotes regional cooperation on a broader scale and at a higher level. By integrating their development strategies, countries can conduct pragmatic cooperation in industry, agriculture, human resource development, green energies, and environmental protection, and turn their resource strengths into driving forces of development.

没有贫困的人类命运共同体

中共十八大以来，习近平提出构建人类命运共同体的重要思想。这一重要思想的内涵极其丰富、深刻，其核心就是中共十九大报告所指出的，“建设持久和平、普遍安全、共同繁荣、开放包容、清洁美丽的世界”。即从政治、安全、经济、文化、生态等5个方面推动构建人类命运共同体。这一思想的提出顺应了历史潮流，回应了时代要求，凝聚了各国共识，为人类社会实现共同发展、持续繁荣、长治久安绘制了蓝图，对中国的和平发展、世界的繁荣进步都具有重大和深远的意义。

事实上，每个国家在谋求自身发展的同时，都应秉持命运与共的理念，积极促进其他各国共同发展，推动各国和各国人民共同享受发展成果。世界长期发展不可能建立在一批国家越来越富裕而另一批国家却长期贫穷落后的基础之上。只有各国共同发展了，世界才能更好发展。习近平在2015减贫与发展高层论坛的主旨演讲中指出，消除贫困依然是当今世界面临的最大全球性挑战。未来15年，对中国和其他

A Poverty-Free Global Community with a Shared Future

Building a global community with a shared future is a profound vision advocated by Xi Jinping. He described the core idea in his report to the 19th CPC National Congress in 2017 as "to build an open, inclusive, clean, and beautiful world that enjoys lasting peace, universal security, and common prosperity." This echoes the historical trend and call of our day, provides room for consensus, and presents a blueprint for human development, sustainable prosperity and lasting peace. It is of far-reaching significance to China's peaceful development and global prosperity.

China stands up for sharing the fruits of development among all countries and peoples. Every country, while pursuing its own development, should actively facilitate the common development of all countries. There cannot be sustainable development in the world when some countries are getting richer and richer while others languish in prolonged poverty and backwardness. Only when all countries achieve common development can there be genuine worldwide development.

Xi Jinping pointed out at the 2015 Global Poverty Reduction and Development Forum that eliminating poverty remains the biggest global challenge, and the next 15 years will

发展中国家都是发展的关键时期。世界要凝聚共识、同舟共济、攻坚克难，致力于合作共赢，为各国人民带来更多福祉。正因如此，他提出了“着力加快全球减贫进程，着力加强减贫发展合作，着力实现多元自主可持续发展，着力改善国际发展环境”四项提议，并呼吁，携手共建一个没有贫困、共同发展的人类命运共同体。

be critical for China and other developing countries. He called on the world to build consensus and join hands to tackle difficulties for win-win results and benefit all peoples. He proposed accelerating global poverty reduction, enhancing cooperation, promoting diverse, independent and sustainable development, and improving the international environment for development, in order to build a poverty-free global community with a shared future.

图书在版编目（CIP）数据

中国关键词．精准脱贫篇：全二册：汉英对照 / 中国外文出版发行事业局，当代中国与世界研究院，中国翻译研究院著；韩清月译．-- 北京：新世界出版社，2020.11

ISBN 978-7-5104-7140-7

Ⅰ．①中… Ⅱ．①中… ②当… ③中… ④韩… Ⅲ．①中国特色社会主义－社会主义建设模式－研究－汉、英 ②扶贫－研究－中国－汉、英 Ⅳ．① D616 ② F126

中国版本图书馆 CIP 数据核字 (2020) 第 221936 号

中国关键词：精准脱贫篇（汉英对照）

作　　者：中国外文出版发行事业局　当代中国与世界研究院
　　　　　中国翻译研究院
翻　　译：韩清月
审　　定：徐明强
改　　稿：David Ferguson [英]
责任编辑：孔德芳
特约编辑：申　阳　赵如意
责任印制：王宝根
出版发行：新世界出版社
社　　址：北京西城区百万庄大街 24 号（100037）
发 行 部：(010) 6899 5968　(010) 6899 8705（传真）
总 编 室：(010) 6899 5424　(010) 6832 6679（传真）
http://www.nwp.cn　http://www.nwp.com.cn
版 权 部：+8610 6899 6306
版权部电子信箱：nwpcd@sina.com
印　　刷：天津旭非印刷有限公司
经　　销：新华书店
开　　本：880mm × 1230mm　1/32
字　　数：200 千字　　印　　张：11.875
版　　次：2020 年 11 月第 1 版　2020 年 11 月第 1 次印刷
书　　号：ISBN 978-7-5104-7140-7
定　　价：78.00 元（全二册）